The Faith of a Surgeon

BELIEF AND EXPERIENCE IN THE LIFE OF
ARTHUR RENDLE SHORT

Edited by
W. M. Capper and D. Johnson

Exeter
The Paternoster Press

ISBN: 0 85364 198 6

AUSTRALIA:
Emu Book Agencies Pty., Ltd.,
63 Berry Street, Granville 2142, N.S.W.

SOUTH AFRICA:
Oxford University Press,
P.O. Box 1141, Oxford House, 11 Buitencingle St., Cape Town

Made and printed in Great Britain for
The Paternoster Press Ltd., Paternoster House,
3 Mount Radford Crescent, Exeter, Devon,
by Redwood Burn Limited, Trowbridge and Esher

Contents

Preface

A short biography of *Arthur Rendle Short: Surgeon and Christian,* which appeared in 1954, gained a very favourable reception. A reprint became necessary in the following year. A number of readers expressed particular interest in Prof. Rendle Short's autobiographical comments and his approach to the Christian Faith. The following pages, therefore, aim to place the emphasis upon his views rather than the details of his life. His own notes, entitled 'My Road to Faith', are the basis of this volume.

Although he had fully indicated his preferences, the joint-author, W. Melville Capper, did not live to see the completion of the present book. Those acquainted with Bristol between the years 1946 and 1970 will be aware of the extent to which he had become the professional and spiritual successor to Prof. Rendle Short. His own challenging autobiography has been published under the title *Questions Colleagues Have Asked Me* (Christian Medical Fellowship).

Acknowledgements have been made at the close of the volume, and it is sincerely hoped that no one who assisted has been overlooked.

D. J.

CHAPTER 1

A Unique Personality

You must be like a promontory of the sea,
against which, though the waves beat continually,
yet it both itself stands and about it are those
swelling waves stilled and quieted.

Marcus Aurelius

A doctor in Bristol telephoning to a close friend in the North of England in the evening of the 14th September 1952, began: 'I have bad news. Professor Rendle Short died suddenly today'. A few minutes later the bell in the North rang again and a voice from the exchange said apologetically, 'When I was transferring the long-distance call, Sir, I could not help overhearing your friend's first words. I am deeply moved. I feel as if I have lost my own father. I grew up in the St. Phillip's ward of Bristol. If ever there was a Christian, that man was. Some of us owe everything to him. He made my father a Christian'.

As soon as the news spread, there were many others who were aware that the city had lost far more than one of the outstanding surgeons at the Royal Infirmary and a distinguished member of the staff of its university. They would no longer be able to consult that versatile mind which for over fifty years had worked with unusual single-mindedness and industry for their spiritual good. Arthur Rendle Short was a man apart. This was not so much from the distinctiveness of any one virtue, but from the unique combination of so many enviable qualities in one person. It is, therefore, important to make clear at the outset what it was which attracted the interest of so many of varied outlooks, social types and religious convictions.

Bristol

Rendle Short was born in Bristol and, except for a short

period in the London medical schools and medical service in France during World War I, spent all his life there. He retained a civic pride which he could not disguise. Gentle boasting about things done 'Bristol fashion' was amongst his more endearing foibles. He could always be relied on to enlarge on the history of the city and to leave no visitor in two minds about its contemporary claims to fame.

He belonged to that small circle of outstandingly able men who have risen from early years of financial stringency to a leading place in their profession and community, but who have never lost the common bond with their fellow-citizens. The neatly frock-coated surgeon of Clifton up on the hill was never happier than when down on the level of his Thursday night meetings with the men of the St. Phillip's ward. One who appeared at times intellectually withdrawn from the common rut revealed, whenever opportunity presented itself, an intense love of children. They were quick to detect this and respond. The wide variety of the human response at so many unexpected places is one of the main interests in the following chapters.

Place in British Medicine

Rendle Short's public reputation, of course, primarily rested upon his outstanding performance as a surgeon and a teacher of surgery. His flair for accurate diagnosis, at a time when there were few technical aids for this difficult art, was a byword in the local medical circles. As for his powers as a tutor to medical students, the *British Journal of Surgery* in a series entitled 'Great Teachers of Surgery' comments, 'In each generation of surgeons there have been some who appeared to be pedagogues by nature. They could not help imparting knowledge ... Amongst those who were pre-eminent in the use of the Socratic method of question and answer, few carried it through so patiently and persistently as Rendle Short of Bristol ... His essential interest in teaching was that every student passing through his hands should come to a clear understanding of the bedrock essentials.'

In several directions he was one of the pioneers in medical research and medical writing. From his teaching post in the Department of Physiology in the University he was one of the earliest of the surgeons to advocate the later applications of physiology to the practice of surgery. He retained a research-orientated outlook throughout his life, and at a later period was a leader in what is now termed 'geographical' pathology. In spite of his busy clinical practice his industry was such that he remained the surgical co-editor of the *Medical Annual* (a volume summarising current advances in diagnosis and treatment) for over thirty-three years. He also produced for his medical publishers – what was perhaps the most difficult of their four monumental 'Index' volumes – *The Index of Prognosis*. An acute mind was yoked to a capacious memory. An ability to penetrate a host of detail and to pick out the essentials was wedded to a historian's grasp of the background. Love of truth and an interest in all phases of scientific investigation were allied to a robust common sense, giving him balance and simplicity.

Religious and Philanthropic Interests

In association with Rendle Short's life-time of conscientious industry in his chosen profession there was found an almost equal capacity for work in the spheres of religion and philanthropy. In most men such a combination would have proved distracting or disastrous to one or other element. But, in his case, his life has an engaging unity. It was all of a piece. At one and the same time – after his professional work had been conscientiously done – he was a very active religious leader, a busy lay preacher, a writer of a considerable Christian literature, a generous philanthropist, and a genius in practical organization. This would have been impossible apart from his capacity for accurate work with a minimum loss of time. Even less could it all have been sustained had there been no adequate factor unifying thought and action into an efficient and satisfying whole.

One dominant strand ran consistently through Rendle Short's life from the beginning to the end – his deep religious faith. It was cast in the mould of nineteenth-century evangelical Protestantism. In this he was influenced by his own father, to whose preaching he never tired of listening, and by George Müller, the Christian philanthropist of Bristol. Sincerely believing that all aspects of life – both professional and private – were equally to be held in trust as a stewardship from God, he enjoyed a virile single--mindedness the fruits of which he sought constantly to share with others.

As a result, his influence was widespread, deep and lasting. Reference has already been made to his stature in the world of medicine. His broader scientific and theological interests qualified him to play an important role in helping Christians, especially Evangelicals, to achieve a mature and rational understanding of their faith which took account both of scientific discovery and the authority of Scripture. In this respect he exercised a decisive influence on many Christians, not least upon students, some of whom were later to extend his work in Christian apologetics.

His life-long association with churches within the Brethren movement was equally productive. His intellectual range, personal devotion, practical wisdom and depth of commitment exerted an influence all the more remarkable in that it did not – and, in the nature of the case, could not – derive from his holding any position of centralised authority.

Less superficially apparent, but no less significant, was his involvement in missionary activity. The missionary study class movement for which he was largely responsible was of great educative importance and aroused many young people to a life-long interest in mission. His personal concern for missionaries and missionary candidates found expression not only in prayer and counsel but in sacrificial giving.

In all these ways, Rendle Short 'being dead yet speaketh'. Mention must also be made of his direct influence upon individuals. Colleagues, students, members of the Shaftesbury Institute Bible School and of the congregations and conferences which he addressed all witness to the quality of his personality and to the transparent fact that the public figure was above all a disciple of Jesus.

‡ The name 'Rendle' was derived from Polperro. A carefully preserved copy of *The Cornish Times*, May 17 1933, provides a description of the historic features of Talland Church, several miles to the East of Polperro. The account concludes with a reference to a succession of learned Parish Clerks from about 1660 until about 1830. Thomas Rendle became Parish Clerk about 1661 and he was succeeded by other members of the family until well into the Nineteenth Century. Members of the Rendle family also held office as Churchwardens on many occasions between 1670 and 1827. One of the bells hung in 1773 bore the name 'Edward Rendle'. The quills of members of the family were constantly in demand by others in the parish when they wished to send important letters. They became known as "the clever Rendles". One descendant, Alfred Barton Rendle, M.A., D.Sc., F.R.S., became Secretary of the Linnaean Society 1916–1923 and President 1923–1927.

CHAPTER 2

Early Years

*To my mind the best of life is something definite
to accomplish, a certain course to run, plenty of
difficulties, and perhaps a spice of danger in the
way, and the certainty that there can be no stop-
ping or relaxing till the end is accomplished.*

H. R. Bowers

Arthur Rendle Short – known as 'Rendle'* in the family –
was born on 6th January, 1880 at 2 St. Michael's Terrace,
Bristol.† His home was situated at a short distance from the house
in Paul Street, Kingsdown, where George Müller (1805–1898), the
philanthropist, who left such a deep influence on the city, was then
living. It is a circumstance which is of more than passing interest.
The connection of his parents with Müller's Homes, and their
friendship with this remarkable man of faith, is essential to any understanding of Rendle's character and outlook. It is also interesting
that his earliest home was a short distance from the Royal Infirmary in Maudlin Street, where he was destined later to work.
Indeed, it was quite possible that the original building could be seen
from his home. He, with his family, would have passed it each Sunday on their way to their church.

Family Background

Rendle himself gives interesting accounts of his grandparents. 'My mother's father, Edward Rendle,‡ was born, and
spent his boyhood, on the borders of Exmoor, above Minehead.
Some of my most vivid childish memories are of his farm called

---

* In the following pages it is proposed for shorter reference to follow the family's
practice of calling him 'Rendle'. But later, from the time of his appointment as Assistant
Surgeon to the Bristol Royal Infirmary, the initials 'A.R.S.' will be used.

† When settled in professional practice, he lived at 90 Queen's Road, and then for
the rest of his life at 69 Pembroke Road, Clifton.

Greenway, on the outskirts of Bristol. He loved his beasts, and to
see them ill-treated was the only thing that ever roused him from
his usual easy-going good temper. In early manhood he had come
under the influence of George Müller, and joined his church.

'The other grandfather, William Short, lived well past eighty
years. He had earlier been a schoolmaster in a Lincolnshire village,
with a schoolmaster's habits and outlook. He used to give me a
shilling for a good school report, though his store of shillings was
never plentiful. He had read George Müller's books, and had been
so impressed that he had come to Bristol to take up a teaching post
in the Orphanage. I am grateful to both these old gentlemen. To the
one I owe a love of teaching and reading; and to the other that
sense of joy in the countryside, especially the lonely countryside,
and all things living in it.'

Philanthropic Interests of Parents

For years Rendle's father, Edward Short,* and his wife
devoted themselves energetically to Christian and philanthropic
work in the city of Bristol. There is an erroneous impression that
Evangelicals have been so interested in the culture of their own
souls that their social influence has been negligible. But the truth is
that, in the last half of the eighteenth and the first half of the
nineteenth century, the Evangelicals were in the vanguard of social
reform, and they have never ceased to interest themselves in such
matters. Some of the most energetic, practical and selfless
philanthropic work in Britain has been that of men in the
Evangelical tradition.

Edward and Katherine Short also had that practical turn of
mind which gets down to the work while others are discussing what
should be done. Their thoughts turned to the need for education
among the city's children. 'Ragged Schools', as they were at that

---

* Rendle's father, Edward Rendle Short, was a man of deep religious faith. He
later became clerk to the directors and head of the office staff in Fry's, the well-known
firm of chocolate-makers. As he progressed in the firm, Edward Short was asked to
become responsible for a brief morning service of prayer which, in the Quaker tradition,
had been organized at the factory. He had the great asset of a fine, ringing voice which he
used to good effect in this gathering at the beginning of each day. The older members of
the staff at Fry's long talked of this and his dignified manner as he read part of a chapter
from the Bible and prayed extempore for the welfare of the whole working community.
Aware of his duty and responsibility, he had taken special care to train for this task. Only
a man with a superlative tone and control of his voice could have held the attention of an
audience of some two thousand men and be clearly heard though they were all standing
on the same level.

time called, had become a feature in a number of the industrial towns. It was therefore not surprising that Edward Short – ably supported by his gifted wife – was for forty years virtually the leader of a Ragged School, known as 'Wagg's'. The superintendent was comparatively illiterate, and he leaned heavily on his better educated co-worker. It proved to be a fruitful partnership. Over one hundred children were under their educational influence each Sunday afternoon until secular authority took over the teaching of the 'three R's'. Wagg's was then able to concentrate upon spiritual and moral instruction.

But this was not all. Edward Short's practical genius – and perhaps even more that of his wife – soon began to direct his attention to the lack of recreational activity for young adolescents during their free time on a Saturday night. These were times when ill-regulated public houses were powerful forces for evil in our cities. For years they visited on week-nights the homes in the parish of St. James. They gave much time to what is now called 'rehabilitation', being tireless in their efforts to renew self-control in notorious drunkards and to provide alternatives to the attractions of the streets. They would return to their home in the small hours of Sunday morning, after organizing a supper and entertainment, at which their own excellent voices – as well as those of invited experts – would be used to good effect. Nor were their efforts merely palliative. Their major aim was that of prevention. Edward Short had an exquisite humour and human qualities which went far in endearing him to down-town Bristol.

Rendle's mother – an effective speaker in women's meetings – also took a deep interest in the Salvation Army. She gave years of service to the auxiliary section known at the time as 'The Slum Dorcas'. Rendle's own later interest in the Shaftesbury Crusade can no doubt be traced to the work of Christian welfare which had claimed so much of his parents' time. He understood the men of St. Phillip's and, what is more, they understood him.

The centre of spiritual influence in the family's life was that of the Assembly of Christian Brethren* at Stokes Croft, Bristol. Here Rendle's father served as an elder and came to exercise a central influence in the whole community. Each week he would preach at least once, often twice. Throughout his father's life the son always listened with deep respect to his preaching. He would fre-

* See Appendix II, page 153.

quently advise students and other young people to take every opportunity of hearing this 'truly Christian man, who can always be counted upon to have some wise thing to say'.

Early Education

Rendle was apt to lament that he had 'nothing to be proud of in his schooldays'. His parents were not well-off financially, and later he had to make his own way on scholarships. At the age of five he attended a 'dame' school in Cheltenham Road. From eight until fourteen he was at Redland Grove College, from which he secured a Bristol City Scholarship to the Merchant Venturers' College. He remained there until he was sixteen and a half. It should be added that taking the same course was his cousin, Helen Case, whom he was later to marry. At the end of his last year at Merchant Venturers, he passed the London Matriculation Examination at the earliest possible age, and was awarded a City Scholarship to University College, Bristol. There can be little doubt that the necessity for securing scholarships served to develop his excellent memory, powers of concentration, and capacity for close work. At a later stage these were to stand him in good stead.

He has left a number of comments on his early education:* 'The Schools I attended were of poor quality. It was, of course, past the days of frequent floggings and gross bullying. There was no ill-treatment to poison the memory. But the teaching was uninspiring, and I remember nothing of the games. Only one of my school-fellows has made any mark in the world. It was my own particular friend, Harry Devine, who later became a distinguished psychiatrist.

'One of the schools had at that time the misfortune to have a headmaster who was equally unpopular with both staff and boys. He had a habit of creeping quietly along corridors outside classrooms, suddenly opening a door and peeping in, waving his hand down, crying "Don't rise, please, don't rise", and vanishing. Masters regarded this trick as spying, and hated it. On one occasion the English master taking the Matric class was demonstrating various methods of forming the past tense, and wrote on the board in English, "The year has passed", and, then, the French "L'an est passé". In came the H.M., produced his usual performance and

---

* The extracts here and subsequently quoted, unless otherwise stated, are drawn from Rendle Short's autobiographical notes left in MS form.

was gone. Our master cast a disdainful glance at the closing door, turned to the board, and altered *l'an* into *l'âne!*†

'On another occasion a Winchester jar of strong ammonia had been dropped and smashed on the stone floor of a storeroom of the chemical laboratory, so the door was kept shut till classes were over for the day. The H.M. came in to inspect the laboratory, and, suspicious as usual, made a bee-line for the closed door. I can see now the watching eye of the Chemistry master, known to us as "Wily Ike", following him. No one said a word. The Head went in, to come out in a few seconds weeping copiously and retreating precipitately.'

Leisure Pursuits

Of Rendle's recreations during adolescent years we know comparatively little, except that he was specially keen on cricket. His chief out-of-door pursuit seems to have been walking which, at a later stage, was to serve well his growing interest in natural history. His walks took him to the Durdham Downs and the Avon Gorge. Later he would go further afield to the coast between Portishead and Clevedon, to the Mendips and the Cheddar Caves and Gorge. When he began to study geology at University College such journeys were always to the accompaniment of a hammer in his pocket and boxes in which to carry home his rock specimens.

From the very first he was a formidable reader. His capacity for absorbing knowledge taxed the resources of his parents to the full. On the non-scientific side his favourites were *The Pilgrim's Progress* and *Holy War* of Bunyan, *Westward Ho!, Hypatia, Lorna Doone,* and the novels of Sir Walter Scott. His partiality for Bunyan's books remained with him for life and, next to the Bible, these retained the highest place in his interest. Apart from his scientific reading, his main interest was in archaeology and history.

The Family Holidays

We have his own account of the earliest holidays. They followed a pattern which he later adopted for his own family. They would visit the remotest places where walking was the chief exercise and observation of nature in all its phases the main object. As a relative once remarked, when declining an invitation to join the family on a holiday, 'The Shorts' only idea of a holiday is to walk

† 'The ass has gone'.

themselves blind!' Recalling these days in later life he wrote: 'Some of the happiest and most vivid recollections of my youth are of our fortnight's summer holiday. There was not enough money, at any rate in the earlier years, for anything elaborate. We loved the lonely places. During the late 1880's there were one or two visits to Newquay. It was then a mere village and the Huer's house was still in use for the "watcher" to cry "Hu" when a shoal of pilchards or mackerel appeared in the bay.

'Then we discovered the country around Hartland. It was fourteen miles from a railway station. There were scarcely any houses or farms at which to stay, and the beaches were too narrow and rocky to attract anyone who wanted comfortable bathing, or sand-digging for their children. But it was grand scenery, and really lonely. We could feel a legitimate grievance if another party was so intrusive as to put in an appearance on one of our beaches. Best of all was Shipload Bay. The cliffs were 400 feet high and there was no proper way down. There was a sheep path, but the sheep did not particularly want to reach the beach. The last fifty feet of the descent was therefore a rough scramble. At the top of the further cliff falcons could often be seen. When we visited the district forty years later the casts of a bird of prey were still to be found at the same point.

'It may be doubted whether our mother shared our enthusiasm for these remote holidays. Catering was often difficult. I remember arriving at dusk on our first visit to one district, at a very dark farmhouse ringed with trees. We could hear the death-watch beetle ticking behind the walls. We were served with milk in a bedroom jug, and cream was abundant. For transport there was a donkey and chaise, but the donkey had notions of his own. He had a habit of rushing for the gate of his own field and standing there, refusing to budge. He would look round to see who was to do the driving. If his master was about his behaviour was exemplary.

'I think perhaps the event of my boyhood that lingers in my memory as the funniest took place in Ilfracombe High Street. There was a china shop on the side nearest the sea, and beneath the shop front there was a window opening into the cellar underneath. Two big dogs had a furious difference of opinion on the pavement and it culminated in a savage fight. One dog backed violently against the cellar window. It broke, and he was pushed by the other dog right through into the cellar. He there fell a considerable height on to a pile of crockery. We could hear crash after crash as he tried to roll off. The irate proprietor descended the cellar steps to deal with the beast which had broken his window and smashed many shillingsworth of his goods. But what really amused us was the cheerful satisfaction of the other dog who had pushed him in. Eyes sparkling, mouth open, tongue hanging out – if ever we saw a dog laugh, that was the occasion!'

Early Religious Education

It is the fashion today to belittle the principle that there is an inheritance of godliness as well as its obverse.* Too many appear lightly to dissipate the birthright that has come from their Christian homes. Rendle made no such mistake. He accepted his spiritual heritage and his subsequent career speaks eloquently of the use which he made of it. The chief spiritual influences which came to him were simple. They came naturally into the family circle by his father's readings from the Bible and prayers, morning and evening. In this way the words of Holy Scripture unconsciously sank into his retentive memory. It was a family joke that at an early age he told one of his aunts, 'I know everything in the Bible, except Ezekiel's dream'. He absorbed the faith of his father almost imperceptibly so that he seems not to have noticed any particular crisis of conversion. At least, he never referred to it.

The family worshipped at Stokes Croft Chapel. On July 20, 1890 in the register of the Sunday School are two new entries – No. 1358 Arthur R. Short, 57 Belvoir Road, aged 10; and No. 1359, Latimer J. Short, aged 8.† Rendle was later a member of the Young Men's Bible Class. At the services at Stokes Croft he would often have heard some of the leading figures of the Christian Brethren in the West Country.

In particular, he would frequently listen to the Sunday morning discourses of George Müller, of world-wide reputation, who at that time divided his ministry between Bethesda Chapel in Great George Street and Stokes Croft. The former was a fine old spacious building standing at the foot of the slopes of Brandon Hill below the Cabot Tower. It was the parent congregation of the

* Exodus 20:5, 6; 2 Timothy 1:4.
† Rendle had one brother. Latimer James Short, after training as a chemist, later took up Medicine at the Bristol General Hospital. He qualified M.B., B. S. 1908, M.D. (London) 1910, M.D. (Bristol) 1911, and D.P.H. 1911. He was later appointed the first Tuberculosis Officer for Somerset. He died in 1976.

Christian Brethren in Bristol from which a number of others subsequently developed in other quarters of the growing city. A booklet found amongst Rendle's papers reproduces an address given on July 6th 1932 by his father on the occasion of its centenary. In 1832, the chapel, then standing empty, had been taken over by Mr. George Müller and Mr. Henry Craik, whose effective biblical expositions had begun to attract the attention of Christians in the city. The numbers swelled, and subsequently a number of gifted men became associated with it. The congregation became the centre of support for Müller's Orphan Homes and for the stream of Christian missionaries which have subsequently gone to many parts of the world on the same principle of 'faith in God', making no appeals for money.

Mr. Müller was an expert in selecting a particular verse of Scripture as it stood in its context, and imprinting it upon the minds and hearts of his hearers. In Müller's Bible, which has been preserved, a text can be seen to have been almost obliterated by his fingermarks. He would press the tip of his finger into the page at Psalm 50:15, and would say to his audience 'You see, I know *God*'. In most other men, such an assertion would have been presumption. But when through prayer alone, and without any appeals whatsoever, a man has had over one million four hundred thousand pounds sent to him for the care of the otherwise untended orphans, we may accept his statement with a profound humility. Here was surely a man who really did know God.

We may be certain that there was no more interested listener in the congregation than one small boy as the preacher would emphasize again and again the secret of his spiritual strength – simple faith in God. Rendle mentioned to a friend on one occasion the thrill it was when the slight figure of Müller would come across the Chapel at the end of the service in order to speak to his parents and himself. On one such occasion, Mr. Müller placed his hand on his head and said: 'God bless you, my boy, and make you a blessing to others'.

CHAPTER 3

Medical Training

Success depends on attention to detail.
Joseph Lister

University College, Bristol, at the turn of the century, had not the dignified buildings which now adorn the University in Queen's Road. We can imagine, however, after the somewhat indifferent opportunities for learning at school, how glad Rendle must have been when he first entered the Science Faculty of the College in October 1896. He was to prove one of its most loyal and fervent supporters in the days ahead. He would later devote to its Medical School the best years of his life.

As earlier mentioned, Rendle gained a scholarship to University College in the October of 1896 and started on the General Science course, in preparation for going on to the clinical medical course in one of the hospitals. At this time University College, Bristol, was affiliated to London University and the students received external London degrees. The College became of full university status granting its own degrees in 1909. After three years in the college, at the early age of 19, he secured the London University B.Sc. degree with First Class Honours in Geology and Physiology, and was awarded a further scholarship. He entered the Bristol General Hospital in 1899 and, a year later, passed the (London) Intermediate Medical examination with a first class in each of the subjects Anatomy, Physiology and Materia Medica. He was also awarded an Exhibition and Gold Medal in both Physiology and Materia Medica.

A Geological Interlude

His references to these years contain much of interest. 'During the second, third and fourth years of my medical studies I took a science degree course in Geology as a side line. It was a whimsical thing to do. Anatomy and Physiology are exacting subjects, and it involved spending an extra year over them, in spite of the financial strain. The motive was partly the inherited love of the country-side, partly the fact that in those days Geology was a subject taken by very few. But my principal reason was that I was interested in the controversy that was being waged between the theologians and the scientists.

'The venture paid handsome dividends. I obtained a B.Sc. with first-class honours in Geology, but that was a small matter compared with firsts in the other subjects. The extra year's study of Anatomy and Physiology enabled me to obtain scholarships, which paid for my clinical studies. and to pass the primary examination for the F.R.C.S. Best of all, acquaintance with the rudiments of Geology has lent interest to every country walk, from that day to this. Fossil-hunting has given me some happy hours. I well remember when I was about twenty-one, being dropped at the end of a rope, to the anger of the local inhabitants, over Aust cliff to find fossils *in situ* for purposes of a paper, read to the Geological Society at Burlington House, on the zoning of the Rhaetic in England.

'I was very fortunate in my teachers. We were taught by Principal Lloyd Morgan and Arthur Vaughan. Lloyd Morgan was a striking personality. Strange to say there was another gentleman – named Sleeman – living in the same part of the town, who was so like him that he was generally known as the "Pseudo-Lloyd Morgan".

'Vaughan, who was writing a London D.Sc. thesis on the zoning of the Carboniferous Limestone, was the best teacher of any subject it has ever been my happiness to meet. He took immense trouble to help us in the study and recognition of fossils. There were no books that covered anything like the same ground. I remember, eight or nine years later, when I was up for my final F.R.C.S. examination, which is the gateway to Consultant Surgery, I thought that I had bungled one of my operations in the practical. Filled with gloom and despair I betook myself to a scientific library and got down a copy of the *Quarterly Journal of the Geological*

Society containing Vaughan's paper on the Carboniferous. It was immensely comforting. Fortunately the examiners did not take such a poor view of my surgery as I did, but that fact did not emerge till later.

Medical Studies

'When I joined the Bristol Medical School, it was with a view to obtaining the ordinary medical qualifications. The later ambition to be a surgeon had not yet begun to make itself felt. Probably that is true in the case of the great majority of junior medical students who may later specialize. On the day that I joined the school Greig Smith, who had become a household name, was buried, at the early age of forty-three. He was one of the three most distinguished men who have, to quote a modern phrase "put Bristol on the map" in medical circles. The others were Hey Groves and Carey Coombs.*

'The Medical School in those days was somewhat primitive. There was, as yet, no university in the city. The dissecting room was warmed by a huge fire at the end of a long apartment. It was a great source of amusement to us to put a row of stools to hot up as close to the fire as possible with their seats nearest the flames, and then to replace them at the tables as quickly as possible just before the anatomy class came out of the lecture and proceeded to their dissecting!

'The students, about a dozen to each year of entry, were not a bright lot. It is true that the tide was beginning to turn since the days of the hard-drinking, ill-disciplined young medicals of the Victorian period. There were a number of very decent, high-principled fellow-students, a few in each year, to whom I owe a great deal, but some were very different. During the South African war, there was a very stormy "Peace" meeting held in the local Y.M.C.A. hall which was attended by a party of students in anything but a peaceful frame of mind. They formed a kind of fort with chairs against one wall and had to be carried out, after a very lively fight, by the stewards, with much damage to the chairs. The last of them, a doughty fighter commonly called Piggy (I don't know why) was allowed to walk out unmolested. The next day one of the stewards came up to the casualty room to receive attention

* J. Greig Smith was a General Surgeon at the Royal Infirmary, and E. W. Hey Groves and Carey F. Coombs were respectively Orthopaedic Surgeon and Cardiological Physician at the General Hospital.

for damage, stared at the dresser on duty, and exclaimed, "*You were the bloke wot broke my jaw last night!*" However, they agreed to let bygones be bygones, and the jaw was duly attended to.

'Eventually I finished with Anatomy and Physiology for the time being, and commenced clinical work at the Bristol General Hospital. Life completely changed. One now began real medical work, and the course was no longer so academic. Also, it became necessary to adjust oneself to working with women as well as with men, and at that particular hospital the ward sisters and Matron ruled the roost. The nurses, too, even down to the most junior, enjoyed a considerable degree of independence.

The Lighter Side of Hospital Life

'During the six months of their studies, medical students lived in the hospital for a week at a time as resident dressers, taking meals with the house medical officers. As there were only two of us, we each spent three months in residence. It was hard work, but a magnificent practical training. At that time dressers were expected to undertake duties that have since, very rightly, been placed on more experienced shoulders. Patients who came up in the evening to have teeth extracted, as many did, came under the dresser's hand. If they wanted an anaesthetic, they must come up by day to the dental clinic. This emergency dentistry was a part of their duty that new dressers hated. I remember one big fellow saying to the patient, as he picked up the extraction forceps, "Well, I've never taken a tooth out before, but I'll make a ghastly effort." The patient ran for his life!

'Some of the sisters were more friendly than others, notably the two who presided in the Casualty Room. Two of the housemen were courting one of them, and both of the suitors' photographs stood on her mantelpiece. We could tell which of them had called on her last because the photo of the other would be turned to the wall!

'The dragon was Sister Fry.* Tall, stout, hard-faced, sixty or so, she terrified us dressers, and was reputed never to be content with the day's work till she had reduced a probationer nurse or two to tears. She shouted across the wards to call public attention to anyone's follies. Even the visiting staff stood in considerable awe of

* Sisters were called not by their surnames, but after the name of their wards.

her. So did her patients! I remember one poor man, told by the out-patient surgeon that he must come in again for another operation, sweating and saying, "Well Sir, I don't mind the operation, but if only you could put me into another ward, Sir. That there Sister do terrify me." He had our sympathy. She was very efficient in her cold way and kept her ward spotlessly clean, and the floor well polished. Some years later she fell heavily on her own polished floor and sustained such a severe fracture that it brought her active career to a conclusion. I fear that there were those who thought it a case of poetic justice.

'The nurses were very friendly but — in those days — there was a risk of trouble from the appropriate authorities if a student were to be caught talking to one of them. A long poem circulated, of composite authorship, a few verses of which still stick in one's memory. They are typical of the outlook.

"If your constitution's iron
And you would in wisdom grow
If you're more than half an angel
Come to us and be a pro.

Should the mid-day meal consist of
Slice of hippopotamus
Turn not up the scornful noselet
Things like this are good for us.

In the silent midnight watches
Do not let your eyelids close
For the emerald-clad Night Sister
Softly comes, and softly goes."

'There were of course courtships, serious and not so serious. I remember one day chatting to another student at the entrance to the operating theatre. He had rather a soft, almost feminine, voice. The telephone rang. He answered. "Is that you, darling?" "Yes". "Are you alone, darling?" Murmurs of assent. "All right. I'm coming up." On arrival the caller was much disconcerted to find no "darling", but two hilarious fellow students!

'When I was one of the resident medical officers a little coterie of about seven lively nurses got it into their heads that I was engaged. This was not far from the truth, but that was not for them to know. They each sent me an effusive *billet-doux* of congratulations. I blush to mention the response, but truth must be told. I bought seven little wedding cake-boxes, imprisoned in each of them a cockroach collected from the multitudes in the kitchens, and addressed the little packet, carefully closed, to each of my correspondents. There were no doubt reprisals. I do not, however, remember what they were.'

A Fortunate Escape

During his years in the Medical School, Rendle had what must have been a very narrow escape from drowning. The incident is best related in his own words.

'Dr D. S. Davies, the enthusiastic and admirable Medical Officer of Health for Bristol who taught us Hygiene, took a party of about a dozen students in the Port Authority launch for an expedition down the Bristol Channel to Flat Holm Island, in order to view the Crematorium there. It was intended, also, no doubt to give us a pleasure trip and we greatly appreciated it. But on the way out someone attempted to turn off a tap which regulated the engine's cooling system, and it broke. The paint on the funnel came out in blisters as a result of the excessive heat of the furnaces. It was decided to call the trip off and return to Portishead, but the coal was being consumed at such a pace that we had not enough to make it. There was nothing for it but to anchor in the middle of the Channel on a submerged sandbank, let the fires out and allow things to cool down sufficiently to enable temporary repairs to be made. So we lay in midstream for a couple of hours.

'Someone suggested a bathe, and most of us, dispensing with the usual attire, went into the water from the dinghy. We had not, however, reckoned with the strength and speed of the current in the Bristol Channel. The tide was sweeping in fast. My swimming powers never did amount to much, and I had really no business to be out at all in these deep waters. My companions quickly regained the safety of the boat, but I was carried far away up stream. I well remember seeing Aust Cliff in the distance and wondering how many miles away it might be. Dr. Davies, who had been watching us from the launch, told me afterwards that he had given me up for lost. However, one of the seamen was in the dinghy and with the aid of the students rowed after me and eventually hauled me in, pretty exhausted. By that time the launch was a long distance from the dinghy and it was a hard pull to regain it. They had to take up the anchor and let her drift to meet us. I was not as frightened as I ought to have been because the boat never seemed to be very far away, though we were being carried along so fast.

Transfer to London

'Before taking the final qualifying examination I took the unusual, but I am sure the wise course, of putting in three months at another hospital, so as to profit by the teaching of a fresh set of physicians and surgeons. I went to University College Hospital in London. The experiment was a great success. It would, of course, have been just as useful for a London student to have spent three months in Bristol. The abundant clinical material and the opportunity of "doing things" would have repaid him well.

'But all this cost money, and expenses had to be cut to the minimum. My first landlady was of the starve-the-cat variety. My meals were scanty and she was an adept at economizing on gas. One had to walk a very long way to save a penny on the 'bus. It was quite a grievance. My colleague Sparkes and I had to search for a place at which to get the cheapest lunch. It had to be situated not far from the hospital at the top of Gower Street and to give us sufficient sustenance to make up for our inadequate suppers.

'An evil spell seems to have been cast over my Bristol fellow-students. Parsons, with whom I studied Geology, joined the Geological Survey of Ceylon, went alone into the jungle, and was never again seen alive. A skeleton, with a geological hammer near it, was eventually found. It was surmised that he had died of snake-bite. J. E. Sparkes developed tuberculosis, half-recovered, and went as a missionary to Central Africa. But the disease recurred and he was soon dead. Other men who shared my final medical studies, J. D. O. Calcott, W. J. H. Pinniger and A. W. C. Richardson, all died of tuberculosis of the lung shortly after qualification. It is a matter for sombre reflection that so many medical students in their sixth year, or doctors just qualified, develop this disease. Although conditions have vastly improved, the risk is still there.'

Growing Academic Distinction

At this point we may well pause to notice the growing evidence of academic distinction and achievement which was already attending him. From University College Hospital in 1903 he had gained the London M.B., B.S., with a scholarship and Gold

Medal in both Medicine and Materia Medica and First Class Honours in Obstetrics. As he also later received the Gold Medal in M.D., there was some substance in the quip of his contemporaries that here was a graduate 'who had enough medals to make his wife a gold necklace'! In other words, spurred by his father's financial difficulties and the realization of the need for gaining as many scholarships as possible, he applied himself to his work to such purpose that he had taken first-class honours in every subject for which he had sat, and at each stage had been awarded a gold medal, and either an exhibition or scholarship.* Such was his success and the understandable anxieties of his hapless fellow-competitors that shortly after his final examinations the senate of University College adjusted the regulations to prevent brilliant 'omnibus' students from carrying off more than their fair share of the spoils. Suffice it to say that, at the end of his career, as a medical student, he had won some £600 in scholarships, paid for all his training, and even finished with a balance in hand.

Those triumphs in the field of learning were not without detrimental features. Success easily begets jealousy. To his contemporaries at this time he appeared conceited and smug. His avidity for knowledge and his tremendous powers of concentration, together with the struggle for financial security, had left its mark, a mark which in the easy-going, somewhat lackadaisical, student world of his day was not likely to be passed over. No successful student is likely to be popular, and especially if that success involves long hours of application to books and the burning of midnight oil. Perhaps it was one of Rendle's deficiencies – and one of which he was aware – that he lacked ordinary bonhomie. He was not a good mixer and lacked the capacity to put the men of the world quickly at their ease.

The religious circle in which he grew up also influenced him powerfully in this respect. The Brethren of those days impressed upon their members the dangers of what they termed 'worldliness'. They also emphasized the duty of spending as little as possible on oneself in order to give liberally to Christian missions and various charitable projects. It was a severe school of self-discipline, but Rendle was a willing pupil. Everyone in his year expected him to pass his examinations with ease – how could he fail? But who

---

* A list of Rendle Short's academic honours (all of London University and the Royal College of Surgeons) will be found in Appendix I, p. 152.

could prophesy in that summer of 1903 that this somewhat introverted serious-minded young man was destined to be a leader of men? Such eventually proved to be the case. It was, however, not through academic competence, but through the sheer moral force of his character bent to a single aim. As Christ said – 'If therefore thine eye be single thy whole body shall be full of light'. Technical competence was soon to have to compete with another ambition.

CHAPTER 4

Hopes Fulfilled and Frustrated

Let me congratulate you on your calling which offers you a choice of intellectual and moral interests found in no other profession and not met with in common pursuits.

James Paget

Having received the basic qualifications for medical practice, Rendle lost no time in securing higher degrees while he was gaining technical experience under expert guidance. Under the former voluntary hospital system, before the National Health Service, 'house' appointments in the hospital were offered, which were posts of conditional responsibility under the control of an experienced physician or surgeon. In return the young doctor — without salary — received free residence at the hospital. In these days of larger staffs, it is difficult to imagine what it was like to work in 1903 as a house surgeon, and to visualize the changes which occurred while the comparatively new principles of aseptic surgery were being applied.

Bristol's Two Hospitals

At the time Rendle was a student, there were two main hospitals in Bristol. The older, known as the Bristol Royal Infirmary, was founded in the autumn of 1736 with 'Charity Universal' as its motto. It can claim to be the first of the great infirmaries which were subsequently to be developed in other provincial cities. It was built on the southern slopes of a hill near the centre of the city. A second institution, the Bristol General Hospital, was founded a century later in February 1831 towards the south-eastern end of the docks, in what was then the populous district of St. Mary Redcliffe.

The initiative for the building of the General Hospital came from members of the Society of Friends. The founding fathers state that it was 'a well-known fact that the Bristol Infirmary has for some time past been incompetent fully to answer the demands made upon the charity by those for whose benefit it was instituted', whilst 'numbers of their fellow creatures were hourly pining under the visitation of disease'.

There were of course additional reasons. The signs are clear that the Nonconformists and Whigs were restive under the strong Anglicanism and Toryism of the Infirmary. *A Short History of the Bristol General Hospital* by J. O. Symes (1932) tells us of one, Dr. Kentish, whose 'enthusiasm in forwarding the foundations of the new hospital was probably not entirely free from political bias for he was a strong Whig and President of the Anchor Society in 1828. Politics entered very largely into the life of the times and the Infirmary was a stronghold of Toryism'. Certainly as late as 1900 the Free Church students were still tending to attach themselves to the General Hospital rather than to the Infirmary.

Resident Appointments

Rendle, having been trained at the General Hospital, started the first of his resident appointments there in the summer of 1903. He held a six months' appointment as Assistant House Surgeon, followed by a period of six months as Casualty Assistant House Surgeon, and finally nine months as House Physician. His testimonials reveal that he 'on several occasions acted as Senior Resident Officer', i.e. in the absence of the Senior Resident. The Senior Physician comments, 'He is the most distinguished student that we have had at the Bristol Medical School during my twenty years' connection with it. I think that with his undoubted abilities Dr. Short is bound to do well in any position in which he is placed, and he should have a very distinguished career before him. It is hardly necessary to add that he is of untiring industry – a quality by no means always combined with intellectual power.'

Following the completion of his duties at the General Hospital he applied for and obtained the post of House Surgeon to the Senior Surgeon at the Bristol Royal Infirmary. He held this more important post until November 1907, and during the last part of this time he combined it with being the Senior Resident Officer.

Return to London

He writes: 'After two years at the Infirmary the time came

to leave in order to return to London. I found it a big wrench. Three months were then spent at the London School of Tropical Medicine, since it was my intention to go abroad. I had the privilege of sitting at the feet of Sir Patrick Manson, one of the pioneers of tropical medicine and an impressive teacher. The course was interesting, and I have always been glad I took it, though the opportunity to put the instruction into practice did not subsequently arise. I received the Diploma in Tropical Medicine on 10th April 1908. I had also simultaneously been taking courses of postgraduate study at Guy's Hospital and St. Bartholomew's Hospital and obtained the F.R.C.S. in the June of 1908.

Appointment to the Royal Infirmary

'On returing to Bristol I became Surgical Registrar at the Infirmary, combined with a part-time teaching post in the Physiology department. It proved a barren period, financially and professionally. A Registrar's work at that time was mainly to keep and index the notes of the patient's case-sheets, and to deputize for members of the surgical staff in their absence. There was little surgical work to be done. The post was unpaid. My total earnings for several years only amounted to about £200 a year, principally derived from privately coaching students for their exams. It was a very bad system. No hospital could hope to secure the services of the more active type of young surgeon to build up its staff if the possible candidates were expected to do virtually no surgery for several years after completing their period of training, and, in the meantime, to support themselves as best they could. The hospital would have paid for a cab to take me down for the occasional night emergency operations, but I usually cycled because I could not afford sixpence as a gratuity for the driver!'

Rendle continues his account of this early period of his medical career with numerous sidelights on the characters and foibles of the colleagues under whom, and with whom, he worked.

'The Infirmary has been fortunate in its records. A hundred and twenty years ago one of the surgeons, Richard Smith, made a priceless collection of spritely stories about the older physicians and surgeons, several of whom were men of outstanding personality. This material, with much more from other sources, was cast into a *History of the Bristol Royal Infirmary* by another surgeon, Munro Smith, in 1917. Most hospital histories are very dull reading, but this is the exception. It presents a wonderful picture of the social habits of the physicians and surgeons of a provincial town in the eighteenth and early nineteenth centuries.

'I found the atmosphere at the Infirmary considerably different from that at the Hospital. The latter was run by the women; the Infirmary was run by the men. The Matron, Miss Baillie, was dignified, competent, and popular. The Sisters were much younger and changed fairly frequently, always excepting Fanny and Julia Gross who had been there longer than anyone could remember, but had not been spoiled thereby. Fanny, in the theatre, was getting a little out-of-date and set in her ways; but Julia, the Sister for the women's surgical ward, was as good as ever, and a pleasure to work with. Her patients loved her. These two sisters had come up from the time when the training of a nurse was rough and spartan indeed. Julia's arm was scarred all over, for she had often given snippets of skin to her patients for purposes of skin-grafting. I offered some of mine to one of her patients one day. It was refused with some asperity. I was surprised, and asked her why. "Well", she told me, "these people have an idea that if the donor becomes insane, so will the receiver!"

'Every Saturday at mid-day all the surgeons, house-surgeons and dressers made a tour of the wards to consult on any cases of interest. Originally, the qualified men wore their top hats on the round, and when a student got his degree or "Membership", he was invited to bring his hat. This custom was killed when one of the sticklers for tradition tripped over the steps down to Ward XIX and his hat rolled into the ward.

'Anaesthesia and surgery were steadily improving. Our very competent, conscientious and modest anaesthetist, A. L. Fleming, who became one of my best friends, had pioneered the method of open-ether with great success. Antiseptic surgery had given place to aseptic surgery, and we now wore gloves and masks. There were certain differences in the type of case that filled the wards. Fractures were treated by the general surgeons, and in large numbers. Modern ambulatory methods for fractured legs were not in use, so that orthopaedic patients stayed in a long time. Results were not good. When a number of surgeons each treat a variety of cases, the results will never be as good as when a few surgeons specialize on some particular line, and have ample experience of this speciality. This can, of course, be over-done. There is danger that the specialists may fail to see the patient as a whole and concentrate on one of the features, which may not be the principal trouble. Frac-

tures, at any rate, present a clear-cut issue. We had many tuberculous glands of neck, tuberculous joints, and tuberculous bone
disease, which are seldom seen in a general hospital today.

'There was a curious ritual with regard to emergency
operations. It was my duty to ring up each surgeon on the staff and
ask if he wished to be fetched. Then a cab would go round, collect
as many as were coming, the surgeon on duty being the last to be
called for. There would be a consultation, then operation, then
coffee in the house-surgeon's room. Paul Bush, the Senior Surgeon,
loved these occasions, and would stay long after midnight. Fortunately, acute appendicitis was not so frequent then as it is now
and there would only be two or three night emergencies in a week.'

Engagement and Marriage

In 1905 Rendle became engaged to his first cousin, Helen
Case, but because of her nursing training, and the unpaid nature of
his hospital appointments, they were not able to marry until the
19th December 1908. The wedding service took place at Alma
Road Chapel, Clifton and was conducted by Mr. G. F. Bergin and
Pastor J. L. Stanley. The former of these was at that time one of
the Directors of Müller's Orphan Homes. One of the hymns sung
was 'O Jesus, I have promised to serve thee to the end', a fact to
which he made frequent reference when asking for this hymn in
later years.

Writing later during the First World War from a casualty
clearing station in France on June 22, 1917, he makes clear the
deep satisfaction which he derived from his marriage:

'... The roads are thick with greasy mud, but as the
weather cleared tonight I got in a bird-walk with Munro...' (Many
letters from France describe the birds he had seen). 'I was spec-
ulating yesterday why we have been so happy over these eight and
a half years, when some married folk aren't. It is scarcely enough
to say we loved each other, because with some folks love goes
up like a rocket and comes down like the stick ... It is partly
because we both had a settled purpose to live godly in this present
evil world. The love of Christ constrains us. Partly because we really knew each other, and there were no serious cross-purposes such
as religious or political differences. But none of these, nor all
together, are sufficient to save some people from being miserable.
There is a something else, a sort of key-fitting lock that cannot be

attributed to mere chance or our own human foresight, but to the predestination of God.

'No doubt we used to think and write like this 9 or 10 years ago, like other lovers, but we have more right to do so now. It is partly in you and partly in me. Why *you* have been happy with *me*, I cannot tell; I know it, and am unspeakably thankful for it ... I can easier find the reasons why I have been happy with you.'

The Rendle Shorts set up their home in Bristol. Whenever he was not engaged on one of the hospital staffs, he acted as locum tenens to various practitioners in the Bristol district, and also coached medical students. These continued to be years of considerable financial stringency. Yet he would frequently and gratefully refer to the lessons which he learnt during this period.

Appointment as Assistant Surgeon

At last, the beginning of several possibilities leading to consultant status opened up. 'In 1913, I became Assistant Surgeon to the Bristol Royal Infirmary. The office was unpaid, but it was the bottom rung of a good ladder. Two surgeons left in quick succession when they reached the ridiculously low retiring age of 55, and, as a third was nearly always ill, I soon had the privileges reserved for a full surgeon, though nominally only an assistant.'

For A.R.S., gaining his full surgeon's status must have been a tremendous relief. He was thirty-three years of age, determined and intrepid, physically robust, mentally alert, and well-equipped in every point for the work ahead of him. Surgery for him was no self-imposed task, but an absorbing interest, into which he put the full complement of all his succeeding years of energy and study. He used to say that his work was to him as interesting and delightful as his recreation. There were busy years ahead, but in them all he never lost his zeal for the practice of surgery, and his love for the Infirmary.

A New Ambition

Another incentive to hard work, in early years deeply implanted in his mind, was beginning quietly, but powerfully, to increase its stimulus. The influence of George Müller, and his infectious interest in world-wide Christian missions, had found its mark. Many well-known missionaries on furlough had visited Bristol or were known in the circle in which he moved. Just when is not known, but it is clear that by the time he was medically qualified he had formed a definite purpose to become a medical missionary. Indeed, it is probable that this intention, consciously or unconsciously, had been the original reason for his taking up the study of medicine. He makes it clear that by the time that he had begun his hospital appointments he had made up his mind to offer for service overseas.

This provides the vital link which enables us to understand how A.R.S. the surgeon is related to A.R.S. the Christian. It explains several enigmas in his subsequent career and puts into perspective what at the time might have appeared an irrational urge to gain certain additional qualifications, for example, the Diploma in Tropical Medicine, at a time when he was engaged in working for his Fellowship of the Royal College of Surgeons. It also explains why he later took up certain local responsibilities and served on several committees which could bring him neither fame, nor money, and might well have hindered his professional success. To be a regular preacher for one of the less fashionable Christian minorities and personally to undertake exhausting philanthropic work is not what one normally associates with the career of a busy surgeon. It certainly is not the way to endear oneself to professional colleagues. There are much easier ways to court esteem.

The fact is that, having failed in three determined attempts to surmount unanticipated obstacles to going overseas, he later devoted himself with characteristic energy to practical support of medical colleagues who were able to go. This was particularly true of the medical men and women who later volunteered for overseas service from the Bristol Medical School. They have had few more ardent supporters at the home base than A.R.S. The spirit in which he entered upon his professional career is aptly expressed by the lines of Thomas Lynch's hymn:

> Dismiss me not Thy service, Lord,
> But train me for Thy will;
> For even I, in fields so broad,
> Some duties may fulfil,
> And I will ask for no reward
> Except to serve Thee still.

It is important to realise that the change from his earlier intention of going overseas as a medical missionary to accepting the status and responsibilities of an Honorary Surgeon of the Bristol Royal Infirmary was for him *radical*. It had the deepest significance for his subsequent spiritual and professional experience. There is little doubt that, had he devoted himself uninterruptedly to physiological research and surgery, he would have reached the very first rank in British medicine.

Offers for Overseas Service

The earnestness with which A.R.S. held to what he regarded as his missionary 'call' and the tenacity with which he had devoted himself to preparation, was brought home to his fiancée at a very early stage by the following incident. In January 1904, whilst still training as a nurse at the Mildmay Mission Hospital, she was suddenly confronted with his question: 'Would you be surprised if I were to be a foreign missionary?' The quick reply came, 'I should be very disappointed if you weren't!' Helen Case had already considered the possibility and was equally set on such a course. She herself had grown up in a home where the family was generous in its support of missionaries. Her father, Mr. Henry Case of Bristol, was one of the responsible leaders in the missionary activities of the Brethren. Indeed she had to make the final arrangements for her marriage, as her father was overseas on a prolonged visit to missionaries in North Africa, whilst the bridegroom was overseas, surveying the possibility of setting up a dispensary in Italy!

During the time that A.R.S. had worked at University College Hospital, London, prior to his entering for the London M.B. examination, he had come into close contact with medical candidates for the various missionary societies who were at the time resident in the hostel of the Medical Missionary Association of London. This Society was founded by Dr. James Maxwell, who had returned from pioneering work in the English Presbyterian Mission Hospital in Formosa. On hearing that he had obtained the F.R.C.S., Dr Maxwell had sought to interest A.R.S. in their hospital in Formosa which was without a surgeon. He offered for this task, but eventually did not go for the reasons he himself has given.*

A little later the couple discussed the possibility of going abroad as Brethren missionaries. Since Helen Case's father was one of the trustees concerned with Brethren workers overseas, they

* See page 41.

naturally expected few difficulties. But, strange as it seemed to them at the time, they did not meet with the ready welcome which they had expected. Mr. Henry Case was opposed, despite his devotion to missions, because he did not think that his future son-in-law's personality and training would readily fit into the type of simple pioneer stations which the Brethren were at that time developing. They were not of the kind which could readily maintain a hospital. They were mainly evangelistic or educational outposts. At most, they could support only a dispensary. A stream-lined F.R.C.S., glistening with medical and surgical efficiency, might find himself somewhat out of his element and frustrated. This impression was confirmed in a final interview with the trustees. They felt sure that he should not go out under their auspices, but encouraged him to offer to one of the larger Christian hospitals which possessed adequate equipment and scope for the type of more advanced surgical work of which he was so clearly capable.

A.R.S. himself, however, resolved to make another attempt on his own to investigate yet further possibilities. He had recently become interested in a remarkable movement under Brethren influence, which had taken place during the late nineteenth century, in Northern Italy. He set off for Naples and neighbouring cities to ascertain if it were possible to set up a hospital, or to practise medicine in some other way. He hoped to assist Italian Protestants, who were battling with the considerable odds posed by an established church which did not understand them and had long persecuted them. He continued this search until the very eve of his wedding in December 1908. The Brethren in Italy, however, were unable to hold out much encouragement. They explained that he would first need to requalify from an Italian university, after acquiring a fluent knowledge of the language, before he could be on the medical register. He, therefore, at length returned to England and married.

The letter fixing the date of the wedding and throwing light on A.R.S's outlook at the time has been preserved. It reads:

'This can only be a line. I have much else to write tonight. It is to be on the 19th. Your father and mine cordially agree that this is the wiser course, all things considered. But this does *not* decide the question of residence. There may be many things to put up with, and likely enough a long struggle with poverty. We may regret that, if we had planned this course more consistently from the first, things would have been much easier. But if we have lost, it is because we *chose,* to try a hard but honourable path for His Name's sake. To the labourer who could only find employment at the last hour, eagerly as he had waited all day, the full penny was given.* He did the smaller work, but he had a willing mind.

'And have we not often said that the height of happiness would be just a small fireside of our own, in our dear old Bristol? We never hoped to be married till September 1908. We are only a few months beyond that date. Ought we not, and do we not in spite of all adverse circumstances, rejoice at the prospect with deep, solemn, reverent joy? I will come to supper at Kingshill tomorrow night after M.S.C. We must now take a trumpet and publish abroad the date.'

Settling to the Home Task

A long weekend in Torquay was all that was spent on honeymoon, and he immediately plunged into a series of locum tenens appointments with general practitioners. They helped to fill in time and to earn a little money while he was waiting for a first appointment at either of the Bristol hospitals. Meanwhile he was still holding himself in readiness for a possible call to overseas service. But the call never came.

Although eventually disappointed by the closing of the doors, he and his wife retained their interest in missionary outreach. They became determined, if possible, to do more whilst staying at home than if they had gone overseas. It was a united effort in the truest sense. They showed their zeal especially by personal example, the organization of interest in missions through young people's societies for this purpose, and finding and helping to equip the right men and women. For over forty years their message to young people was: 'If you are not able to be a missionary for God overseas yourself, then use every opportunity of doing your bit from home.'

* A reference to Christ's parable of the labourers in the vineyard (Matt. 20:1–17).

CHAPTER 5

The Road to Faith

God, stooping, shows sufficient of His light for
us in the dark to rise by ... and I rise.
                                        Browning

The crucial point in the career of A.R.S., came, as we have seen, in 1909. In the light of the subsequent course of his life, the perspective now becomes clear. In private notes made about this time (and subsequently in 1951 when his wife was seriously ill) he took time to express himself with greater self-reference than usual. He has provided us with some of his deepest thoughts in what he called 'My Road to Faith'. Characteristically, he introduced these subjects with a brief apology.

'No doubt some readers may consider the substance of what follows as in the nature of an anticlimax. To leave it out, however, would be to present a thoroughly distorted picture of my life. Men and women must have some kind of faith, philosophy, purpose, or theory – call it what you will – to live by. They may be divided roughly into two classes, (i) those who care for nothing but what an animal cares for, food and drink (especially drink), sex, exercise, fun, love of domination; and (ii) those who live for a purpose.

'The purpose may be worth while, or not. It may be that commonest and most exciting game in the world, money-grabbing. It may be some ardent social theory or hero-worship, such as animated the suffragette campaign, or Marxism, or Nazism, or some other -ism. It may be bird-watching, or chess, or tennis, or stamp-collecting. Or a man may be completely absorbed in his professional work. The doctor stands at a point of vantage here, because his work is varied, full of thrilling human and scientific interest; it presents endless opportunities for further discovery, and it earns the gratitude of other people who find themselves benefited. This is more especially true of consultant practice. And then there are those of us who feel that all these are too earth-bound, they smell too much of the decay and dissolution and disappointment to which the finest brains and the most vigorous bodies all come in the end. *Pulvis et umbra sumus.*

Home Influences

'I was brought up in a home that was Puritan, but happy. The restrictions were made as little irksome as possible, and there were many compensations. The household was profoundly influenced by close touch with as remarkable an adventure of faith as modern England has ever witnessed. A ne'er-do-well young Prussian, George Müller* by name, had experienced one of those dramatic changes of attitude towards God and the world that have sometimes made history, as did for instance the conversion of John Wesley, or of William Wilberforce. He came to Bristol, and became the unordained pastor of an independent church, called Bethesda. The basic principle was to make the rules of the fellowship conform, as closely as modern conditions permitted, to the pattern of the first century church as described in the New Testament. Human innovations throughout Church History were as tares sown amongst the wheat.

'But you cannot make New Testament principles work unless you have men with New Testament faith. George Müller had. Principally to inculcate this faith in other people (but also, of course, from sympathy with the destitute children who had nothing before them except the choice between vagabondage or the tender mercies of the early Victorian workhouse system) he founded in Bristol an orphanage on the singular principle that it was to be supported, as he himself was supported, entirely by faith in God. There were to be no begging appeals. No needs were to be advertised, even if details were requested by intending donors, except that, whether they were in funds, or out of funds, an annual report was issued so as to provide things honest in the sight of all men. No committee was behind the venture.

'The reader will expect to hear that such a quixotic enterprise, run by a young, enthusiastic and almost unknown foreigner, soon came to grief. It did not. True, there were great trials of faith.

* See pages 92–94.

Twenty-three times in two consecutive years they began the day with insufficient funds or food to provide for the day's meals. But funds or food invariably arrived in time. So did helpers; so did buildings. They were supported by nothing but prayer, and the voluntary gifts of sympathetic people who did not know whether they were giving to a cause that was at the moment sunk in poverty, or well provided for. During George Müller's lifetime, about 10,000 orphans passed through the homes. and £1,400,000 was donated.* The orphanage has out-lasted George Müller by over fifty years, and is still run on the same principles, though happily there is not the same bitter need among the children of England as there was at the beginning.

The Impact of Science

'My grandfather left his school in Lincolnshire to come to Bristol and take up a position as master at George Müller's Homes, so it is not surprising that our family was influenced by this triumphant example of faith. But I was cast for an education in a school of science. I do not recollect that chemistry or physics much influenced my thinking, but zoology and physiology and geology did, and disturbingly. Everything was to be brought to the test of the laboratory, to personal observation and experiment.

'It was the era of triumphant Darwinism. Modern doubts as to the sufficiency of a self-working theory of Natural Selection to account for the origin of all living things had scarcely yet achieved a hearing among men of science. Wellhausen's theories about the Old Testament, and Baur's about the New Testament were accepted, even by theologians, as pretty well proven. Some people seem to be able to hold on to religious faith by a process of turning a Nelson's blind eye on conflicting facts and theories. But I was not made that way. I could not follow "cunningly devised fables", however glamorous. Things were moving on to an intellectual *impasse*. Some working hypothesis had to be found, or something would have to be thrown overboard. Fortunately I was preserved from the folly of a precipitate decision.

'It is difficult to be quite sure, as one turns over the pages of memory of nearly fifty years ago, that one correctly evaluates the most significant directives of one's own life. It may be that something really important has been forgotten. But it seems to me,

* At the present value of the pound this would be not less than £4,000,000.

it has always seemed to me when memory was fresher, that there were two inter-twined Ariadne threads to lead through the maze of those most formative years of life, the late teens and the early twenties. One thread was intellectual, and the other vocational.

The Intellectual Strand

'I owed very little to sermons in coming to a conclusion as to whether the fundamental data of the Christian Faith were credible or not. I did not sit much under a scholarly ministry. Even if it were occasionally scholarly, the preacher's education was not as my education, nor his mind as my mind. But I owed a good deal to books. It was my daily habit to read a short portion of the Bible. There were a good many books besides. If I mention some of them, it is purely as a tribute to their value to myself. One ought not to despise the lower rungs of the ladder one climbed by. Those books are more or less out of date now. It should not be difficult to find better. I cannot remember the exact date of finding them, nor the exact order.

'One was Henry Drummond's *Natural Law in the Spiritual World*. I do not think the first reading of any book has ever given me such a thrill. The modern reader will be at a loss to understand this. Now, its science is largely out-dated. But it showed me, for the first time, that a synthesis between natural science and the Christian message was not impossible, and that the Designer of the world might very well be the God of the Christian.

'One day, browsing among books in the Medical Library, I found on an obscure shelf an old volume by W. K. Hobart, called *The Medical Language of St. Luke* (1882). I knew enough Greek to be able to follow it. It was a convincing demonstration, derived from a close comparison of the language of the author of the third Gospel and the Acts of the Apostles with that of the Greek medical writers, Hippocrates, Galen, Aretaeus, that whoever wrote these two books of the New Testament was a medical man. He uses twenty-three technical medical expressions not found in the other New Testament writers. Four of these, diagnosis, dysentery, thrombi, syndrome, have been taken over into modern medical English. There was much in the book besides, of course. I believe present-day opinion is that Hobert proved his case, but somewhat over-stated it. All this started me off on a line of study, with eminently satisfactory results, confirming the early date and general reliability of the four Gospels. This was a little later greatly helped by reading B. F. Westcott's *Introduction to the Study of the Four Gospels,* and his *Canon of the New Testament,* and Dean Farrar's *Life of Christ.*

'But though the Gospels might be written by men of the first century, was the text trustworthy? Here, I had a friend, the late F. G. Bergin,* whom I used to call playfully my "Right Reverend Father in God", who, though a layman, was really interested in textual criticism. He lent me Westcott and Hort's fascinating book on the subject, to which I was later able to add other reading.'

In some of his earliest writing, A.R.S. expressed, tentatively, his views on biblical authority.

'We do not suggest that the approval stamped by the Lord Jesus Christ on the Bible is such as to force our acceptance of every verse in it even if an error could be proved; faith never flies in the face of truth. We are willing to make all allowance for a little uncertainty and inaccuracy here and there in the transmission of the sacred text; and for the fact that revelation is gradual and progressive from Genesis to Revelation, so that neither the morality nor the theology of Jacob or David is on the same plane as that of Paul or Timothy. We admit that tradition is not infallible as to the human authorship of certain books. But we do plead, in view of Christ's attitude to the Book and its own claims, and the moral power and purity of its influence (even when the location of the writer was a sink of iniquity like Rome, or Patmos, or Corinth, or Jerusalem under Zedekiah) that it should be given a fair hearing as inspired of God, and not refused on account of miracle, or prophecy, or contradiction by a secular historian, or some modern literary theory such as the Graf-Wellhausen hypothesis.

'And finally, if the Christian has definitely come to the decision that the Bible is the Word of God for him, what follows but that it becomes his unfailing guide, which must at all costs be obeyed? Whatever his ecclesiastical outlook in the church in which he worships, he must not look for human tradition, or for popularity, or for all that appeals to the intellect and emotions in making his choice, but simply be guided by what the New Testament teaches.

'For us of the modern generation, the distinctions between the various denominations − Anglican, Methodist, or Baptist − which we have inherited from our grandparents are of relatively lit-

---

* Dr. Frank Bergin, son of G. F. Bergin, who succeeded George Müller as Director of the Orphan Homes. He was later Consultant Radiologist at the Bristol General Hospital and lived in Clifton a short distance from Rendle Short.

tle importance compared with the attitude of a congregation of Christians to the historic faith – by which we mean the Gospel of man's redemption from ruin, and regeneration by faith in Christ, and the acceptance of the Bible as the inspired and authoritative Word of God, to which no man has any right to add nor from which the right to take away. The crucial difference between professing Christians today is not related to matters of church government, or ordinances, rather it lies here. Some hold rigidly to the historic faith, and others accept only a modernized version of it which, we fear, neither the great British preachers of the past five hundred years, nor the leaders of the Reformation to which we owe so much, nor the Apostles themselves, would have recognized. We call it crucial, because Jude tells us that the faith was "once for all delivered unto the saints". If so, every man puts himself in the wrong who tries to modify it in any way, whether he be an early Father, or a modern church dignitary. Paul wrote to the Galatians, "Though we, or an angel from heaven, should preach unto you any gospel other than that which we preached unto you, let him be anathema", and to the Thessalonians, "If any man obeyeth not our word by this epistle, note that man, that ye have no company with him, to the end that he may be ashamed."

'The Book will have a say too, concerning a Christian's earthly relationships and moral conduct as a master, or a servant, or a member of a community or family; it will guide as to the use of his time and money and recreations. So the Word of God becomes, as was intended by the divine Author, 'a lamp to our feet', compared with which every human guidance – whether it be an organized church, or a dominant teacher, or our own unilluminated conscience or intellect – is as a will-o'-the-wisp. And we find again, that besides the intellectual decision whether we will believe in the Bible or no, there is a moral choice. Our conception of right and wrong will have to be tested by the Book, and we must act accordingly.

'Another question follows. Granted the records, what ought one to think of the Person whose story they tell? I had read sermons quoting texts showing what the writers of the New Testament thought about Him, but that sounded to me like arguing in a circle. The argument would be advanced that the writers were inspired, therefore their testimony that Christ is a divine Person must be true. Then we know they are inspired because Christ, who is a divine Person, says so – and so on. It was Carnegie Simpson's valuable little book *The Fact of Christ* that broke into the circle. The true grounds for believing in His Deity are to be found in Christ's character. Added to this are His teaching, His practical wisdom, His miracles, His resurrection, and His influence on history. He is too wonderful for the four evangelists to have imagined Him.'

A.R.S. was influential in having *The Fact of Christ* reprinted in 1952.* The evidence of what the book had meant to him in the stabilizing of his faith is provided in the foreword which he wrote to the new issue:

'What a special and peculiar interest there is in revisiting a scene which one used to love, which influenced one's life, which has evoked many happy memories, but which has not been actually seen for years. How eagerly one looks for what is remembered, and for what has been forgotten, for what has changed, and for what has not changed. I feel persuaded that many, like myself, will share something of a like pleasure in reading again, after all these years, Carnegie Simpson's *The Fact of Christ*. To some of them, as to me, it opened up a kind of trunk road of thought. It showed how to find the most convincing evidence that Jesus Christ, or Lord, is worthy of the highest honour, an honour which indeed is quite inadequate if it does not amount to worship. In nothing which I have read since have His claims been better stated.

Here, in an early chapter, the reader is reminded that in His teaching He made Himself, not the truths He announced, the centre of His message. In another chapter it is demonstrated that in Him was no fault visible to His contemporaries, nor inward failure visible to Himself. His purity of holiness, love for all mankind, forgiveness of wrongs suffered, and humility, well exemplified by His readiness to give time and attention to quite unimportant people, were virtues which He introduced almost new into the world. The influence of His spirit on subsequent generations of His followers has never passed away, whereas that of all other leaders of men has soon been dissipated when they are dead. But we will pull no more out from the book. The reader must finish it for himself. We shall be greatly surprised if he is not a better worshipper as a result of so doing.'

'So, by degrees, faith was seen not to be contrary to reason

---

* *The Fact of Christ*, P. Carnegie Simpson, 1952. London. James Clark and Co. Ltd.

– indeed, it is *by faith* that we really come to understand! In retrospect I have merely indicated those best-remembered step-ping-stones by which I crossed the stream. It would take too long to set out in detail here just what I came to believe, and why. Also, it is unnecessary, as I have done so elsewhere, as for instance in my book *Why Believe?*

'An unsympathetic reader may reply that my conclusions were not arrived at by pure reason, but that they were influenced by feelings. But we cannot alter the psychological fact, stated in the words of Carl Jung, that "It is most often feeling that is decisive in matters of good and evil, and if feeling does not come to the aid of reason, the latter is usually powerless". The reader may suspect that, if I had found other books, I might have come to different conclusions. He may even maintain that on account of my early education I was not entirely free from all bias in my (quite sincere) search for truth.

'As a matter of fact it is very doubtful if it is possible for anyone to be entirely free from all bias in seeking to come to work-ing conclusions about God, and Christ, and the Bible, and Heaven, and the last judgment. Certainly the people who decide to dis-believe all these are generally the ones who show their bias most obviously. Some have been brought up in a very religious at-mosphere and have hated it. Others I know of have been sons of men who were ardent Christians of the tactless and too pressing kind who no doubt vexed their sons to distraction. Another was ex-pelled from an important academic position for adultery. Another, a woman, was the divorced wife of a clergyman. Many men and women dare not be Christian. It would interfere too much with their way of living. It is more congenial for them to cherish every argument that can be found against the Christian faith. Why believe in the last judgment if you do not care to face it? But we make no general accusations. Many non-believers are of the most exemplary courage and character. They have often been strongly, perhaps unconsciously, influenced in the direction of high moral standards by the widespread diffusion in the community of those ideas of right and wrong which centuries of Bible reading very hap-pily brought into these islands.

'Christians have often been accused of adopting their faith as a kind of escapism from the unpleasantness and circumscription of their lives. It acts, we are told, like opium, or novel-reading. We are not disposed to deny that the miserable, the degraded, the lonely, the heavy-laden, have in multitudes of cases, in every land, in every generation, found joy and peace in believing. But those who see nothing but escapism fail to recognise the fact that no other faith, religious or secular, makes greater demands for self-sacrifice on those who embrace it.

The Vocational Strand

'There was in my case a second strand in my experience which was not intellectual, but vocational. That is to say, a choice had to be made of a way of life. From my early teens I had built a kind of castle in the air that I might one day be a medical missionary. This idea was probably based on hero-worship. Two aunts had been in the foreign mission field; I had often heard missionaries speak. It seemed a noble enterprise. But when I was well launched on my medical studies and was beginning to do well, and prospects opened out at home, the vision faded and I came to hate the thought of going abroad. It sounded a lonely, squalid, poverty-stricken existence. Foreign travel did not appeal to me in the least. One day, I noticed a text, a quite unfamiliar text, printed on a calendar. It was this: "Seekest thou great things for thyself? Seek them not."*

'There were two men at my hospital, both senior to me, both very well qualified and apparently destined for responsible appointments and brilliant careers. One was H. Stanley Jenkins,† the other R. Fletcher Moorshead.‡ I had many a talk with the latter, and came to a tentative decision to give my life to that kind of work. It was not in a spirit of escapism. I always disliked the prospect heartily. But it seemed the right thing to do. There was a great need, and I was in a position to meet that need, in some small corner of the wide world. So it had to be.

'Yes, but which corner? And under what conditions? That was a problem which went unsolved for years. I wanted a decently equipped hospital where serious surgery could be done. I felt no vocation to go out, as some of my friends did, on what are called "faith lines", without any guarantee of support. Whether this was due to lack of faith, or to divine guidance, I was never able quite to decide. Eventually, after obtaining the Fellowship of the Royal College of Surgeons, and passing through a course in Tropical

---

* A further reference to this and explanation is on page 50.
† H. Stanley Jenkins, Presbyterian medical missionary to China.
‡ R. Fletcher Moorshead, Baptist medical missionary to India.

Medicine in London, definite steps had to be taken. My fiancée and I offered our services to a mission, to go out to join their work in Formosa. Their medical executive committee accepted us. But the general committee turned us down on the grounds that we did not share the views of the denomination on the the baptism of infants. This came to us as a shock and surprise.

'I resolved to try another way. I went to Naples to make plans to go and set up in practice there and do missionary work among university students. A few days in Italy were enough to show that this scheme was quite impracticable. Through those years of exploration and half-formed decisions three texts from the Bible took unbidden possession of my thoughts. "Many are called, but few are chosen." "It was well that it was in thine heart." "Thou canst not follow me now, but thou shalt follow me hereafter."

'Only so much is here related as seems necessary to present a true picture of the significant turning points that go to make up life's direction. Perhaps we do not always correctly estimate our turning points and the motives for decisions, even in retrospect. But I have not consciously suppressed anything material.

A Disturbing Experience

'About this time, there took place one of the most alarming and memorable incidents in my life. For many years it was not possible to mention it publicly, until after the death of the doctor concerned, and indeed the memory was too painful to invite thinking about. When I had just finished my hospital resident appointments, I accepted an invitation to act as locum for a suburban doctor for about a week. It was my first experience of general practice, and a miserable type of practice it was, of the kind which is now almost and happily extinct. Huge crowds of patients flocked to the surgery night after night, Sundays and weekdays. They nearly all belonged to some sick-club or other. It was before the days of the panel. Few of them expected or wished to be examined. What they wanted was a bottle of medicine, and a certificate to go on the club for sick pay so as to escape work for a while. Indeed, they came in such hordes that there was no time to make anything like a thorough examination.

'The doctor was on a holiday, which he no doubt greatly needed. He had left his assistant, a young overseas doctor, and a girl dispenser, to carry on, with my help, All the medicines we ordered came from his own dispensary. During the day, there were visits to be paid. I liked that part of the work, because accurate diagnosis and treatment were possible. The evening surgeries were a nightmare if you had any medical conscience.

'On Sunday evening, the assistant announced that he was going out, and the dispenser did not come on Sundays, So I must myself dispense everything that I ordered. He showed me the untidy little dispensary, and explained that the bottles on one shelf were put up eight times proper strength for convenience of storage, but the bottles on another shelf were of normal strength. "But there is nothing on the label to show which is which," I objected. "Oh, that's all right. The dispenser knows, and we know. I'll be back about 10.30. Good evening." He took himself off.

'I saw dozens of patients. From time to time I called a halt and went to the dispensary to put up bottles of physic. Halfway through the evening I was seized with a spasm of misgiving. Those bottles on that shelf were concentrated, these were normal, but what about this lowest shelf? The labels were quite uninforming. I did not know. I gave no more drugs from that shelf. When the assistant came back, I took him to the dispensary.

' "I quite understand that these medicines are eight times proper strength, and these are normal, but what about this lowest shelf?" I asked. "Oh, they are eight times the normal strength too," he replied. "Well, you didn't make that clear to me," I expostulated.

'As I looked at that fatal row of labels, my heart stood still. One of the bottles contained an opium mixture, and I knew I had dispensed from it twice. Another bottle contained magnesium sulphate: that had been used, too. Worst of all, I had sent out at least one bottle of medicine from a mixture containing nux vomica. The active principle of nux vomica is strychnine, and strychnine poisoning is a terribly painful form of death. Eight times the normal quantity of opium or strychnine would be a fatal dose, and these unfortunate people had been told to take the medicine not once but three times a day. Nor did it seem possible to identify or warn them. They were nearly all strangers to me. No books or records were kept in that practice. We did manage to remember two of the patients, but not till the next day. There was nothing to do but to pray, and that I did long and earnestly. I transcribe the next paragraph from an account, written later for private use.

' "That night, my *Daily Light* portion commenced: 'If thou faint in the day of adversity, thy strength is small.' 'Cast thy burden upon the Lord, and he shall sustain thee.' I slept not at all. But once more that faint, trembling faith possessed me, faint yet quite unmistakable, that all would be well. I regarded, and do regard, this as the strangest of the vicissitudes of those anxious hours. Next day, after earnest consultation, we called on a few possible patients and stopped one or two comparatively harmless mixtures. We sent advertisements to the two evening papers asking all who had obtained medicine at Dr. —'s surgery on Sunday night to return at once. One paper refused to insert it. The other brought no response."

'We found later that the man who had been given the nux vomica mixture had gone to London; the first dose of the medicine had made him sick, and he had thrown the rest away. Another man had taken a dose of the mag. sulph. mixture; he had had a busy night, but there was no harm done, and he took no more. What came to the patients with opium mixtures we never found out. There were no known disasters. What actually happened I do not pretend to explain. The drugs were fresh, and on the Monday morning the dispenser confirmed the strength of the various stock bottles.

'I am not suggesting for a moment, of course, that the Christian has any right to expect that the Almighty will in some semi-miraculous way alter the laws of nature, or protect him from the consequences of his own carelessness, folly or misfortune. But the incident did very emphatically teach me that it is no vain thing to call upon the Lord.'

The Death of Christ

Following closely, as he did, the Bible's teaching, at the very heart of A.R.S.'s faith was the sacrificial death of our Lord Jesus Christ. We find frequent reference to this subject in his writings and addresses:*

'The modern mind hates the thought of being indebted to another's sufferings, but this very indebtedness is strangely bound up with the constitution of things. Modern Medicine and Surgery save many lives and much suffering today, but they have had to learn by the method of trial and error, and success has been dearly purchased. It has cost the lives of countless animals and many

---

* The following extract is taken principally from *The Bible and Modern Research*, pp. 124–126.

human beings, on whom unsuccessful methods of treatment were tried. England is free and at peace today, but she owes it to those whose names are inscribed on the Menin Gate, and in the graveyards of France and Flanders. No child comes into the world without costing a mother something, and the debt only accumulates year by year afterwards.

'All this may help us to understand what our Lord meant when he claimed to die as a ransom for many. Repeatedly He referred to His death: "I, if I be lifted up from the earth, will draw all men unto Me." To Him, it was His death, not His life, not His teaching, that was His master-stroke. No human reformer thinks like this; for him death ends all, even if by it he hopes to influence public opinion. But Christ never refers to the effect of His death on public opinion. He died because an atoning death was the most necessary service He could render the world. The Apostles staked everything on Christ's death, not on His life, and they must have learnt this from Himself.

'It is very significant that although our Lord "took away the sins of the world", He gave Himself a ransom on behalf of all men,* and is the propitiation or atonement on behalf of the whole world yet we are not told in Scripture that He died instead of *all,* but "instead of *many*", and the passages speaking of His substitution are addressed to believers. He suffered *on behalf of* all the world; as *a willing substitute* for believers.

'Such an atonement would have been valueless had a mere man been the substitute. He could but die for his own sins; he could not redeem a lost and guilty world. Christ, who died for us, had no sins of His own for which to suffer.

> "But spotless, innocent and pure
> Our great Redeemer stood."

'He was possessed of the full Deity. His life was not that of an ordinary man, weighing light in the scale against the wickedness of millions. He was the only begotten Son of God, and His life's worth would pay the redemption price for the whole human family a thousand times over − a Cullinan diamond for a heap of common, dirty stones. In the last analysis, it is impossible fully to explain or fully to illustrate this great gospel that God Himself is the

* I Tim. 2:6.

One who has made atonement. It is He who fully knows how He is able to be perfectly "just and the Justifier of them who believe in Jesus".

'Human nature rebels at this teaching, and weak men and women, who have seen evidence enough to convince them of the divine authority of the statements we have quoted, begin to hesitate and to let go the truth. Some have even asked, Would English justice permit a judge to punish a substitute, even a willing substitute, in the place of the guilty person? Can God do so without impairing His justice?

'Those who fail to appreciate the justice of the atonement are often being misled by human analogies or by some inadequate illustration. There are several elements entering into the course of human justice which are lacking when we look at the final judgment of the world. Our law courts exist not only to dispense retribution but also to reform the man who has gone astray, and to warn others against copying his crimes. Before the Great White Throne it will be too late for reformation, and too late for warning.

'When first brought face to face with this claim, the intellect refuses to receive it. If Jesus were really God, and He was put to death, why, something stupendous must surely happen; the universe would disintegrate. We are told that some things did happen. The earth quaked; the sun ceased to shine for three mid-day hours. But no one else died. He died to bring life, not death, and prayed for His murderers.

'Let us write down another fact: Christ staked everything, life itself, on the theory, nay, the certainty, that being God, He could die for the sins of the world. If in this He was mistaken, His life was an enigma indeed.

'Alongside the facts concerning the death of Christ we must consider the claim that He rose from the dead. If this is true, three conclusions follow. The first is, that "He was declared to be the Son of God with power, in that God raised Him from the dead". All His claims were vindicated. The second is, that He is alive to-day. And the third, that a Christian graveyard ceases to be a place of gloom. Christ was the first-fruits of them that sleep "in sure and certain hope of a blessed resurrection".'

The Great Divide

A favourite subject on which A.R.S. would frequently speak to groups of university students dealt with the question: What is the essential difference between the outlook of a Christian and a non-Christian?

'There is only one safe way to know.* It is to take the words of the original exponents of the Christian message, and to collate those statements which plainly tell us. But first, let it be observed that there is a fundamental distinction, a profound line of cleavage, between two ways, two classes of people and two destinies, in Christ's own teaching. He speaks of the broad way and the narrow, the house built on the rock and the house on the sand, the separation of the sheep and the goats, the resurrection of life and the resurrection of judgment, Dives and Lazarus. He makes such radical statements as "Except ye be converted and become as little children, ye shall not enter into the kingdom of heaven." "Except a man be born again, he cannot see the kingdom of God ... That which is born of the flesh is flesh; that which is born of the Spirit is spirit."

'And how may men pass over from the one way, class, destiny, to the other? There are about twenty statements on this subject coming from Christ Himself and recorded in the four Gospels; and another twenty or so, given in the Acts and Epistles, coming from the Apostles, agreeing remarkably with those spoken by their Master. We must not choose some one or two favourite texts that suit our personal views, and neglect the rest; we must give full weight to the whole.

'The statements fall into five groups. There are, first and most numerous, the "believe" passages. It is noteworthy that none of them ask us to believe a theological fact or doctrine, however true and important, but all to believe on a Person.

'Secondly, there are the "repent" passages.

'Thirdly, come those which speak of a changed and purified life, or the acceptance of Christ as Master.

'Fourthly, a few passages requiring an open confession of our faith.

'And fifthly, a few which have been taken to indicate the necessity for certain Christian ceremonies.

'Now we are well aware that many a reader will gaze at this list in consternation. We shall be told that it is far too long and that on this reckoning the way of salvation is too difficult for anybody to understand. We do not think so. Even if the criticism is true, it is

---

* This extract is taken from *The Bible and Modern Research*, pp. 241–246.

safer to include too many texts, than to omit some that may, after all, prove vital. The list is simpler than it looks. The second and third groups of passages, in practice, come to the same thing, for repentance is not only a turning away from the bad past, but a turning to the better future.

'What does "believing" or "faith" mean in the Bible? Faith is not just the solving of a problem. It is the motive and the driving force for living a particular kind of life. "The life which I now live," says St. Paul, "I live in faith, the faith which is in the Son of God, who loved me and gave himself up for me." The great chapter on faith in Hebrews gives example after example of what faith made men do. The words used for "believing" and "obeying" are often transposable.

'And indeed, faith in common life is nothing but a word, we might say a sham, if it does not issue in deeds. The fiancée trusts her fortunes to her husband and shares his life. The pilot risks all by going up in a plane he has investigated and with which he is satisfied. The business man chooses a bank he can trust, and puts his money there. The sick man allows himself to be rendered unconscious while the surgeon in whom he has faith removes some diseased organ from his body. The nation at war entrusts her navy or army to a carefully chosen admiral or general. When we are in real need, we can do no other. We are bound to trust. So with the Christian. There is a sense of need – sin that calls for forgiveness, temptation that makes us cry for succour, loneliness that wants the Great Companion, a future judgment that we dread, and can by no means face without One to ransom us. If some one says he has no such sense of need, the answer is simple; he has never had his eyes opened to the holiness of God, nor to the guilt of human sin. He is living in a fool's paradise, like a man with leprosy or cancer who does not know it. That sense of need makes us put our faith in Jesus Christ.

'He must be received in full character, or not at all. He came as Messiah to the Jews; the Christian accepts Him as such. He came as God to be worshipped; the Christian believes and worships. He came as Lord to be obeyed; the Christian humbly says: "I will follow." He came, as His name Jesus declares, to save His people from their sins, which He did by dying for them. The Christian gratefully acknowledges with St. Paul, "He loved me, and gave himself for me . . ."

'This must not be interpreted to mean that all these elements have to be present and realized, in every conversion. Far from it. In the great majority of cases only one element is present to consciousness; the rest are subconscious, latent. They are unrealized at first; they come to light afterwards. That is why experiences differ so greatly. St. Paul suddenly discovered that the Jesus whose followers he hated and despised was the Lord in Heaven. Augustine became stricken by conscience, and decided to leave his pleasant vices for ever. Luther, climbing the church steps on his knees, remembered a Scripture that the just shall live by faith, not by penances and pious acts. John Wesley at the meeting in Aldersgate Street felt his heart strangely warmed. "I felt I did trust Christ, Christ alone, for salvation, and an assurance was given me that he had taken away my sins, even mine." In other cases there are no well-remembered and dated spiritual crises, especially with those whose experience of eternal life began in childhood. So the door of entrance may seem to us to be painted in differing colours, but it opens on to Christ Himself, the Way, the Truth, and the Life.'

CHAPTER 6

Ambition: Vice or Virtue?

*'Do everything in its own time, do everything in
earnest. If it is worth doing, then do it with all
your might. Above all, keep much in the
presence of God.'*
            R. M. McCheyne

The start of the road had not been without its severe intellectual difficulties. Yet to one of A.R.S.'s single minded temperament these would seem to have been light compared with his vocational problems – the failure of his hopes in relation to overseas service. He felt it far more deeply than he may have shown at the time. One who knew him well writes: 'The late Professor Rendle Short was by some considered cold and unemotional. A surgeon, I suppose, needs to be able to keep a good hold upon himself. But notwithstanding the impassivity of his face he believed strongly and felt deeply and for him there was no preacher like the one who knew how to touch the heartstrings. I recall an occasion when I was sitting beside him at a conference and listening to the late James Stephen speak on the subject of "The World's Need". Stephen was greatly helped of God that night; he shook us all and the atmosphere was vibrant with spiritual power. When the speaker ceased, there was a long tense silence, broken at last for me by the quiet voice of Rendle Short saying in my ear, "This is the kind of thing that makes a man believe in the Holy Ghost".

'He was always deeply moved by this subject of the call to Christian Missions. When a speaker at another of the conferences had appealed for recruits for overseas service, it was observed that Rendle Short openly dabbed his eyes with his handkerchief, and afterwards said to a friend; "It was I who asked him to take that subject, but when he did so, I found that I just couldn't stand it . . ." '

The recurrent evidence of a substratum of emotion in relation to this matter may explain the many occasions on which he spoke to students — and especially postgraduate students on the threshold of their careers — concerning the subject of "Ambition — Vice or Virtue?" The full notes of one such have been preserved. We see from it how fully he had come to terms with the problem in his own life:—

The Searching Question

'Is ambition un-Christian? This was the question which suddenly loomed up in the mind of a medical graduate who was well known to me, a good many years ago now. He had obtained first-class honours in his university degree examination. He was just about to sit for a higher qualification, the first of a series for which he had laid his plans. If he were to be successful, which seemed not unlikely, a career as a specialist was assured. But one morning on a daily text calendar he read these words: "Seekest thou great things for thyself? Seek them not." It was like a blow in the face. He did not even know that there was such a verse in the Bible. Was ambition wrong? Ought the Christian to be content with a pass degree and an ordinary career? Is it true that ambition is "the last infirmity of noble minds"?

'Obviously, the first thing to do was to investigate the text. It records words spoken by Jeremiah to his secretary Baruch. Their little world was falling to pieces around them. Jeremiah saw this plainly; Baruch, with the optimism of youth, not so plainly. It would lead only to disappointment for him to sketch out an ambitious place for himself, when everything was about to swirl down into dissolution. We think that we live in a different and much more stable world. The text does not apply. But do we? "The fashion of this world passeth away." "Seeing that all these things shall be dissolved, what manner of persons ought ye to be?" These divine messages would be just as true, even if shadows did not hang over Europe and the Far East and if the economic position of Britain were as secure as it was in the days of Queen Victoria.

'After a few weeks' consideration, the graduate took another look at the text and two words, at first almost unnoticed, stood out. "Seekest thou great things *for thyself?*" Self-centred amibition is undoubtedly an infirmity, and the minds that are guilty of it are not even noble as a rule. Nebuchadnezzar, Alexander of Macedonia, Julius Caesar, Pope Innocent III, Napoleon Bonaparte, and Hitler:

these were ambitious men, and their ambition brought misery to thousands. Big businesses have been built up by ambitious men by cut-throat competition, and their unsuccessful rivals have had to fight for the crumbs that fell from the rich man's table. It is a very serious thing in a school or university to have to work alongside a clever, scheming colleague who is full of vaunting ambition.

'Christ's twelve disciples had a jealous eye on their personal position and prospects. On the most solemn occasions they were struggling for the first place, even at the Last Supper. Again and again the Lord had to rebuke them. He told them, when they were bidden to a feast, to sit down nearest the door and not at the high table.

Justifiable Ambition

'There is an ambition which is Christian. It does not seek for the things which the world considers stable and attractive, but which we know are scheduled for demolition, like the great stones in Herod's temple. It does not seek great things that would be used only for self and not for service to Christ. Here are some examples of an Apostle's ambition: "I press towards the mark for the prize of the high calling." "So run, that ye may obtain." "It is required in stewards, that a man be found faithful." "Study to show thyself approved unto God, a workman that needeth not to be ashamed." "Whatsoever thy hand findeth to do, do it with thy might."

'With considerations such as these before us, let us come back to the man who is seeking to improve his position, perhaps by embarking upon some specialist career. He evidently needs to ask himself some searching questions and to answer them quite honestly. Is he going to be bitterly disappointed and angry with the Almighty if he fails? (Of course, if the failure is due to his own laziness, he may well be upset.) Will this coveted position be used for the glory of God, make him more useful in Christian service? Or will it merely increase his own importance? Is he being fair to his colleagues? Is he laying up his treasure on earth or in heaven? We are not saying for a moment that a position on a university staff for instance, a managerial post in a big firm, or unusual skill at a game are to be despised as adjuncts to Christian service. They may well be talents which God can use for His glory and for the futherance of His work. Some have to take the lead, but they need not be conceited about it. On the other hand, it may not be His purpose to give us prominence, or wealth, or wide influence. It is for

Him to distribute gifts as He will. We may have to play second fiddle, and a very difficult instrument it is to play well. But the man in the parable with two talents achieved as rich a reward as the man with five.

'If success comes, for example, in the form of a higher degree, we may well consider that it is not in the same category as the "great things" that Baruch was not to seek. It is the outward and visible token of an inward and invisible competence, or would be if examinations were a reliable guide, which is true in only a very general way. That is to say, it is evidence that the candidate has been working diligently and has acquired skill and knowledge which he is anxious to use for the benefit of the community. He has been "not slothful in business". It is one way to serve the Lord.

Where Care is Needed

'It is not only sons and daughters who need Christ's sober teaching on the subject of ambition. Parents need it too. How many a son or daughter has been ruined by an ambitious parent who manoeuvred a worldly marriage, or sent a son into a business that was profitable to the purse, but deadly to the soul. There is a story in the Gospels illustrative of the ambitious parent. It is that of Salome, who brought her two sons to Jesus, and kneeling before Him asked for them the chief places in His kingdom. Did they remember, and did Salome remember, their boasting that they were able to drink of His cup and be baptized with His baptism on those later days when James was slain with the sword and John was beaten in Jerusalem and exiled to the convict station of Patmos? Christian parents, too, must learn to desire the treasures of heaven for their children, rather than the treasures of Egypt, or they may incur a terrible responsibility for spiritual disasters.

'There is another form of ambition which it may be well to mention, because those who cherish it often do so unconsciously; that is, the ambition to dominate the lives of other people. The parson, the doctor, the teacher, the owner or manager of a business, the head of a government office or department, are specially liable to succumb to this temptation, because so many persons come to them for advice or direction. All the well-known Scriptures which exhort us to humility, to look not only on our own things but also on the things of others, are meant to warn us against this love of domination. Absolute power over other people corrupts the best and wisest. The record of the latter years of Solomon, king of

Israel, furnishes a striking example of this. It is an ambition we are not likely to have pointed out to us, so that it is all the more important that there should be ruthless self-scrutiny, best undertaken when we are young enough to check the fault before it becomes second nature to us.

" 'Give me neither poverty nor riches; feed me with food convenient for me; lest I be full, and deny thee, and say, Who is the Lord? or lest I be poor, and steal, and take the name of my God in vain.' "*

The Use of Money

A detailed analysis of the situation which confronted A.R.S. soon after he had completed the Final Examination for the F.R.C.S. was found amongst his autobiographical notes. He had the custom of recording his prayers and analysing his major motives, and from these we learn of the self-discipline which he found necessary when academic honours were rapidly falling to him. That the early resolve to see that all 'pecuniary benefits' were taxed for the service of God was actually kept, is seen from the record of the total value of gifts between 1909–1915:

'In regard to our financial affairs, our settled income was only sixty pounds a year at first, and often we could only see our way for a few weeks more. The wolf was only just round the corner. I do not think that we were ever afraid that the Lord would forget to provide. Just now our financial difficulty is greater than ever and we do not see any hope of improvement. Teaching has fallen off very seriously indeed, and private practice shows no sign of increasing. We have been able to give away more than the Lord's tenth up till now and to lay by a little. But the future is uncertain and we simply wait in faith and patience till God shall lead us in His own way. In March 1912 I had to withdraw thirty pounds from the deposit account. Private practice and teaching up to May was almost nil.'

(November 1912). 'Financial supplies, both by operative work and teaching, have continued abundant and we have more than paid back the thirty pounds to the deposit.' He kept up the practice of tithing his income throughout his life. Later figures show that his aim was to exceed the basic 10% 'tithe', and the more so as his income increased.

* Pr. 30:8, 9.

The following is a record of gifts to Christian work and charities:–

	Income £	Given away £
1909	225	26
1910	323	42
1911	312	16 (not complete)
1912	327	25
1913	463	69
1914	698	86
1915	1,341	250

The Use of Time

A further sidelight on his views concerning the difficult question how to balance one's duty to God and duty to one's fellow men comes at the close of an address to Christian students on the 'Use of Time'.

'It often happens in life that two or more duties seem to pull us in different directions. The Christian, during the brief years that he is an undergraduate in a university, nearly always experiences such a pull. His studies, and the necessity to work hard to pass examinations; the claims of home (especially for women students); games and social activities; the exhortations he receives demanding time for Christian service both within and outside the walls of the university – these all call for time, and are all a good use of time. But the twenty-four-hour day simply is not long enough. To increase the day by reducing sleep can be overdone. The old adage says: 'Nature wants five, custom gives seven, laziness nine, and wickedness eleven.' But very few moderns, living at the pace we do, can keep their brains bright on less than seven hours, and many need half an hour more.

'It is most important to regard time as a God-given stewardship, just as money is a stewardship. That is to say, it is definitely wrong to waste it; it is misappropriation of goods. One day we shall have to give account of how we have used time, because it is not ours, but God's. So let us look through our day and its doings, and see if we think He is likely to approve.

'It is extraordinarily easy to waste time. We leave gaps in our programme, too short to fill with anything important, but longer than is necessary to ensure punctuality at our next appointment (not that punctuality is one of the writer's shining virtues). This

wants watching. It is most valuable to develop a really critical conscience on this subject. Granted that, late in the evening, perhaps,
we may be too tired to do anything but relax; nevertheless during
the working day let us remember the substance of another old
adage: 'Lost, somewhere between sunrise and sunset, one golden
hour, set with sixty diamond minutes. No reward is offered for its
recovery; it is gone irretrievably.'

For a student one most difficult decision, as a rule, is how
much time to give to Christian Union meetings, Christian service
and to outside church work, against the background of academic
studies. On the one hand, parents* have invested a certain amount
of money in providing an education for their son or daughter, and
have every right to expect reasonable dividends in the shape of examinations passed at the correct intervals. If the student is paying
his own expenses this argument has less weight (he may think it has
more weight); but it is no advertisement for the cause if Christian
Union committee members make a poor show in examinations. I
am no believer in the theory that prayer is an efficient substitute for
work in the matter of degree-hunting.

On the other hand, the Christian admits that God has a
claim on his time for His service. This means that the undergraduate has to decide where that service is to be given and
what proportion of his time is to be devoted to it. The university is
a little world of its own to which the majority of students have
access only during the few years of their course. Within this community are to be found the future leaders of world thought. Their
minds are open; their interests are wide; many are anxious to discuss the basic problems of life and to find workable solutions for
them.

His Own Use of Time

'All this sounds very theoretical and generalized, no doubt.
To be concrete, may I venture to recall my own practice during the
years of my pre-clinical studies? True, Christian Unions in those
days offered only one meeting a week, and there were few Christian Conferences. But as I lived in the city, there had to be church
attendance every Sunday morning. I preached nearly every Sunday
night, and regularly attended a weekly prayer meeting. There was
also time, on Sundays, for a certain amount of Christian reading,

* Today we must add 'the community'.

which has been of very great permanent value. It was quite possible to give this amount of time, and still do justice to medical studies. It did not, however, leave leisure for much else, except on Saturday afternoons.

'In my own later experience the combination of hospital and private surgical practice, instruction of medical students and post-graduates, attendance on the innumerable committees that a position on a University Senate necessitates, with preaching, both at home and at a distance, has not left much leisure for other things. But I cannot think of any other way of life that I would have preferred to live.'

CHAPTER 7

Physiologist and Surgeon

It is impossible to know perfectly the part, if one is not acquainted with the whole, even in a gross way; so it is impossible to be a good surgeon if one is not familiar with the foundations and generalizations of medicine. On the other hand, as it is impossible to know the whole perfectly if we are not acquainted in a certain measure with each of its parts; so it is impossible for anyone to be a good physician who is absolutely ignorant of the art of surgery, with a knowledge of its possibilities and its limitations.

Henri de Mondeville

The professional career of Rendle Short as a surgeon covered thirty-three years, from his first appointment in 1913 until he resigned from the Professorship of Surgery in Bristol University in 1946. These years were spent in the practice of surgery, teaching, writing, editing medical works, and research. Even before 1913, while still a registrar, he had shown an interest in research. He demonstrated his capacity for original work and writing by producing a number of monographs on widely differing medical and surgical subjects. Soon, however, he commenced to devote his time to Physiology and General Surgery. His medical training and active life as a surgeon falls roughly into four main stages, the first of which has already been described above:

1897–1903 Training Years.

1903–1912 Early Practice and Clinical Research.

1913–1923 Growing Practice: Assistant Surgeon and War Service in France.

1923–1946 Surgeon, University Teacher, Joint-Editor of the *Medical Annual* (summarising current medical and surgical research), and Professor of Surgery.

Soon after qualifying A.R.S. started to contribute articles to medical journals. There is an array of monographs to his credit from this 1903–1912 period. From his application for the post of Assistant Surgeon in 1913 we find that he already had published papers on Actinomycosis of the Appendix, Cutaneous Anaesthesia, the relation between Iodoform and Thyroidism, and Oxaluria. In addition, he collected records of what he called 'end results' of various operative procedures. These findings were published in a number of journals, and include the 'end results' of surgery in epithelioma of the lip, tetanus, ruptured viscera, cancer of the tongue, gallstones, and many other conditions.

The Importance of Physiology

Before he had finished his Registrar's appointment his book *The New Physiology in Surgical and General Practice,* first published in 1911, had already gone through two editions, and had been translated into German. During his preparation for the London M.D. he had been impressed by the importance of Physiology in the day-to-day practice of medicine. It was also during his registrarship that he began to realize the vital significance of the application of Physiology to Surgery. This was undoubtedly stimulated by his appointment as senior demonstrator in Physiology in the University.

A.R.S. remained at heart a physiologist and research observer. He was among the earliest surgeon-physiologists to appreciate the need closely to correlate Physiology with the various branches of Medicine and Surgery. This was well seen in his work on the aetiology of acute appendicitis. In 1911 he read a paper before the Royal Society of Medicine reporting observations on the degeneration and cell changes resulting from sections of the posterior nerve roots in man.

In the preface to *The New Physiology* he wrote that the triumphs of the surgeon were at that time unknown to the physiologist and that the converse was equally true. 'Many of the discoveries of the past ten years which have so changed the face of physiology are fraught with vast possibilities for the clinician. This book is an attempt to sift out from the New Physiology that which is likely to be of value in the actual diagnosis and treatment.' Today, of course, the book has nothing 'new' about it. But, at the time, it was a pioneer attempt to apply physiological facts to day-to-day surgical experience. Especially notable is the contribution on blood transfusion in haemophilia, and iodine in hyperthyroidism.

He lived long enough to see modern Surgery fully justify his attempt to associate the two disciplines of Physiology and Surgery. From earliest times the surgeon has been traditionally viewed as a supercraftsman chiefly in the field of Anatomy, who needed to have all the craftsman's intimate and detailed knowledge of structure. Today, with the realization that function is as important as structure, surgeons are forced to pay increasing attention to the demands of Physiology and the basic sciences. Whilst craftsmanship was ever increasing its finesse, A.R.S. was proud of the definition of a surgeon as 'a physician who operates'.

His fruitful interest in Physiology received a further impetus, when, having been Demonstrator 1910–1914, he was in 1914 appointed full Lecturer in Physiology in Bristol University. He continued to lecture in this department until as late as 1928, in spite of his ever-increasing preoccupation with the teaching of Surgery. In the early days, before private practice was assured, one reason for his pursuing the lectureship was undoubtedly financial. But, also, he was always deeply interested in the subject and deliberately chose to continue with it long after his surgical practice was extensive and lucrative. His mind found its stimulus to research mainly from that direction. Indeed, he continued to write on Physiology until 1948 when he published the last edition under his own name of his *Synopsis of Physiology,* first issued in 1927.

Surgical Shock

It is not surprising that in his Hunterian Lectureship before the Royal College of Surgeons on 'Surgical Shock' on 9th February, 1914, he stated: 'My subject is one of the meeting-places of Physiology and Surgery. These meeting-places are likely in the future to assume more and more importance. Anatomy has been the traditional road to Surgery in the past, but it has almost paid the sum-total of its contributions towards the advancement of surgical science. Physiology, on the other hand, which has grown out of all knowledge in the past twenty years, still stands full of gifts, as the work of the physiologists, like Horsley, Grile, and Cushing has already shown.

'Primitive Surgery had to face four apparently insurmountable barriers before it would fulfil its mission in the saving of human life and the relief of suffering. The first of these was haemorrhage, and the victory had already been gained in Hunter's day. The second was pain. This barrier fell down when anaesthetics were introduced. The third was sepsis, a danger over which Lord Lister showed us how to triumph. The last great barrier to be conquered is shock, and we do not yet see how the assault is to be made. But three victories make us very confident of final success, and we believe that one day Surgery will have lost its main terrors and will be able to bring benefit to patients who are now doomed to die unrelieved; for instance, cases of intracranial or intra-thoracic disease, and what we now call 'inoperable' carcinoma. We may not hope to prevent or treat surgical shock until we have an accurate conception of its nature and causation, and we shall proceed to pass in review some of the suggestions which have been made, and to see how they fare under the criticism of exact experiment. This review will be in a sense the mental autobiography of the writer, inasmuch as he has been attracted by each theory in turn, but on putting it to the test has had to give it up for another.'

A.R.S. modestly closed his lecture by saying: 'The present lecture is as a scout sent forth to survey the barrier and a scout's difficult ambition is to tell a tale which the future will prove true.' He was not to know, of course, that on 4th August of that very year would begin a clash between nations which was to develop into a blood bath in which recovery from surgical shock would be an important factor in survival after wounding. Although the full answer to the problem was not known till the Second World War, his sane assessment of the existing physiological knowledge put before the College of Surgeons in March 1914 was read and re-read, as surgeons had to face the problem of well-developed shock in so many thousands of cases.

The 1914 War

All too soon A.R.S.'s appointment as Assistant Hon. Surgeon to the Royal Infirmary engulfed him in the many day-to-day exactions of modern general surgical practice. The pressures were greatly accentuated by the 1914 war. It was nothing for him to operate for a good deal of the day and then to travel from Bristol to Hereford, or down to Barnstaple, in order to undertake further operating in the evening. He would return in the small hours in order to be ready for work the next morning. At that time he was responsible for nearly all the night emergencies at the B.R.I. as well as being in charge of half of the surgical out-patients and wards.

Throughout the years his steel-like constitution was his greatest asset, next to his retentive and voluminous memory. His day-to-day resilience and physical stamina seemed to need little reinforcement apart from regular food and sleep.

He tells us that 'The out-break of the war made my work very heavy, though not just at first. The illness and death of H. F. Mole left us one surgeon short, two others were sent overseas, and another was given heavy duties around the district which kept him away from the Bristol hospitals. Nearly all the hospital residents were called up, and had to be replaced by students, which made things very difficult. Then a private house, at Bishops Knoll, was given over by the owner, Paul Bush's brother, to be a military hospital. That had to be staffed. Later on, Southmead Hospital was turned into a military hospital also, with one thousand beds. Mr. Hey Groves and other surgeons from the General Hospital did much work at Southmead, but there was plenty to do. The patients were often gravely ill; their wounds suppurated vilely, and we were kept on the run with cases of severe secondary haemorrhage. On three different occasions I had to tie the common iliac artery for dangerous bleeding. I never wish to work as hard again as I did during a period of about a year in 1916–1917. I have a note that I performed 54 operations in three successive days. Nearly all the night immediates at the Bristol Royal Infirmary fell to my lot, with half the surgical wards, and half the out-patients.'

Military Surgery in Flanders

Shock was clearly of importance to the military authorities and not unnaturally he was one of those surgeons who were specially commissioned to go to Flanders to enquire into the treatment of severe shock. He was later given a commission which enabled him to go to most parts of the British front. Characteristically he did a great deal of the travel between field hospitals on a bicycle! Here, again, we have his own account of some of the more interesting features of this period.

'One of our annoyances at this time (i.e. the early days of the war) was false alarms of being required to proceed to France. One night, after notice to go, while all my kit was stacked in the hall ready for tomorrow's departure, the notice was cancelled at midnight. I took a holiday on the Gower Coast; four times the one-legged telegraph messenger lad pursued me on one beach or another with a telegram from the War Office to know where was I;

and was I ready to go if needed? It was scarcely the way to enjoy a holiday.

'All my service in France was at one or other of the casualty clearing stations. First I was with the Fifth Army, near Albert, then at a new C.C.S. in front of Poperinghe, which the troops called 'Dozingham'. There was another nearby called 'Mendingham' and a sanitary station called 'Delouzingham'. After a few months Colonel Gray, chief surgical consultant of the Third Army, arranged without my knowledge for my transfer to undertake the study and treatment of shock in a casualty clearing station of that Army. I was located at Grevillers, near Bapaume, but with a roving commission up and down the front. At this particular C.C.S. there was a pathological laboratory housed in a reconditioned London omnibus, in the charge of a Canadian pathologist named Lindsay, who very kindly allowed me to carry out some researches in his department.

'It soon became apparent that the prostration, often fatal, that followed war wounds, was of composite origin. Most of the patients had lost a good deal of blood, and this was the primary cause of their poor condition. A very important factor, in a large number of cases, was toxaemia from oncoming infection with virulent streptococci, or the organisms derived from manured farm-land, which gave rise to gas-gangrene. Surgical shock, strictly interpreted, means a state of depression of vital functions due to severe injury, apart from serious bleeding or infection, and both in war and in peace is much less common, and more difficult to treat. Our patients were often dying from a mixture of all three. We had no anti-gas-gangrene serum available and it was long before the days of sulphonamides, or penicillin. My pre-war investigations into the nature of surgical shock had not indicated any particularly valuable remedy.

The Earliest Blood-Transfusions

'About this time, though scarcely anything had been published on the subject, we heard that experiments had been made at base hospitals with blood transfusions, though as far as I know, in the summer of 1917, it had not been used at the front-line hospitals. We resolved to try. Methods had to be improvised. At that time we knew nothing about blood-groups, or incompatibilities. A lieutenant, whose leg had been shattered, and who had bled so much that he was pulseless, was our first patient. A donor was obtained and we brought the two side by side, cut down on the radial artery of the donor and an arm vein of the recipient, under local anaesthesia, and joined artery to vein by a short length of rubber tubing with a needle at each end. This crude method was very successful on that occasion. The lieutenant's pulse improved a good deal, the amputation was carried out successfully, and the donor was none the worse for it. We soon discovered, however, that some better technique would have to be found. It was quite impossible to tell how much blood, if any, was passing from donor to patient, except the very rough test of watching their pulses. Or clotting would take place, and no blood at all passed.

'We decided to withdraw a pint of blood into sodium citrate solution to prevent coagulation, collect it in a flask, and carry that to the patient's bedside. This is the method in use today, but our apparatus was crude. First we had to find out whether sodium citrate could be injected without doing any harm. There were some rabbits belonging to the laboratory, and my colleague undertook the test. He injected a huge dose, for a rabbit, of citrate solution into a vein in the animal's ear. It fell over and was obviously unconscious. I thought it was dead, and that the proposed citrate method was going to be too dangerous. However, it picked itself up after a minute or two, solemnly hopped across its pen, and started nibbling at a lettuce in the corner. No doubt the injection had been given too fast. So the citrate method was worth trying after all. Donors were easy to obtain. We promised them a letter to take with them down to the base, to the effect that though their own wounds were not serious they had given their blood and we hoped they would be granted leave to go to England. They raced along the corridor to volunteer, when this became known. There were no mishaps in our short series of early blood transfusions, though we found that the veins of gravely wounded men were sometimes in such spasm that considerable force was necessary to get the blood in. A number of lives were saved, but not, of course, those of patients with toxaemia from gas-gangrene. The pure haemorrhage cases did best.

'At this stage brass hats, or rather the purple hats of the R.A.M.C., became interested. They found and sent up to us a keen young American specialist, named O. H. Robertson, who told us about the four blood groups and the necessity to use a donor of the same group as the patient, or of what was then called Group IV, now Group O, the "universal donor". Nowadays, of course, the position is much more complicated. It was due to good fortune that we had had no disasters from giving incompatible blood. Under Robertson's guidance we resolved to try storing blood in an ice chamber. We knew that the battle of Cambrai was imminent because, however carefully the secret of a new offensive may be kept, the front-line hospitals have to be strengthened. Nowadays either whole blood is stored, or blood plasma without the corpuscles. We stored the corpuscles but discarded the plasma. About twenty pints were prepared within a week of the beginning of the battle; Colonel Gray insisted on contributing a pint himself. We intended to reserve this for a wounded General, but we did not receive any Generals, and I do not know who got that particular bottle. We were overwhelmed with wounded and all the blood we could obtain was needed badly enough.

'It was necessary to lay wounds widely open and to excise the damaged and soiled tissues, as a means of preventing infection, at any rate if the patient was brought in early enough. This of course left a huge gaping cavity and when it was clean, after four or five days, it seemed desirable to draw the sides together. Someone suggested that it would be a good scheme to affix a broad strip of plaster to the skin on either side of the wound, with a row of corset hooks along the edges and use a lace to approximate them. I undertook to go into Amiens, our shopping centre, thirty miles away across thoroughly devastated country, to buy the wherewithal. We liked a trip to Amiens. There were good restaurants there and for twenty francs one could get an excellent dinner at the hotel. It was not till I reached the draper's shop that the real difficulty of my task occurred to me. I did not know the French for corset hooks; indeed my spoken French was very limited. I felt acutely embarrassed and wished I had sent one of our five or six nursing sisters. We managed somehow, but I think mademoiselle was left wondering what on earth a British officer could want with corset hooks!'

Lecturer and Examiner in Physiology

A.R.S.'s lectures on Physiology in Bristol during his years of teaching the subject were models of their kind and his teaching was eagerly sought after. The notes were carefully dictated and recorded by the students. Indeed, he used to ensure that this was so. It was largely as a result of his care to impress on his students the need for good note-taking that *The Synopsis of Physiology*

(1927, in conjunction with Dr C. I. Ham) was written. It had been worked up from lecture notes. 'One of my students, now qualified, had to lie up for a long time after an operation and became very bored. I told her that if I was so circumstanced I should write a book. She replied that she had nothing to write about. By way of helping I said, "You have very full notes of my Physiology lectures; what about working them up into a synopsis?" She did this, though the notes also needed a good deal of expansion by myself before they could be published.'

For some years he was examiner in Physiology for the Primary F.R.C.S. and he tells us:—

'This brought me into contact with a number of distinguished surgeons, physiologists, and anatomists. It was very exacting work; the papers, often eighty of them, had to be read and marked within a few days, in the period between the written and the *viva voce* parts of the examination. This meant very close application and very little time for anything else. Not more than a third of the candidates passed, and many legends had grown up as to the ferocity of the examiners and the out-of-the-way nature of the questions asked. It is true that examiners sometimes had fads, and that they over-rated the importance of what would normally be considered unnecessary information. But, as a rule, the occurrence of hard questions at the end of a *viva voce* examination meant that the examiners took a favourable view of the candidate.

'I well remember one particularly intelligent and well-informed woman student. After the first ten minutes of her viva it was plain that she must pass, so in the remainder of the time I did certainly ask some advanced questions, to see how far she could go. Some she answered, some she could not. As I was firing my final shot, time was up. Quick as a flash she retorted, "I don't know, but the bell's gone!" I was so pleased that I gave her the highest mark of my eight years' examining. I am not surprised that she rose to eminence.

'Occasionally students pass, or hope to pass, examinations by artfulness without information. One of my colleagues, who had written a textbook, used to tell how a candidate, halfway through a viva, when asked something he did not know, wreathed his face into a smile and said "Why, sir, I was reading that in your book last night". He struggled on for another five minutes; then he was stumped again. Another smile: "My luck's dead in today sir. I was reading that up too!" Once more he got away with it, and passed.

Students often hope to pick up information by button-holing candidates who have just come out of the examination room. This can be double-edged. There is a well-known story of a candidate's describing in second-hand details the physical signs of a heart case which his informant had told him was at the end of the row of patients. The examiner heard him grimly through, then remarked quietly, "That patient, sir, is at the *other* end of the row".

'One of my students was an England international rugby player. He told me that, when he was up for his finals, he was required to look at certain microscopic slides and to write down what he saw. Near at hand was an elderly porter, looking like an Egyptian mummy, standing guard. The candidate, after examining the first slide, murmured under his breath, "Epithelioma". "Look again, sir, look again", said a sepulchral voice, coming from nowhere in particular. He did look again, and murmured, "Rodent ulcer". "Put it down, sir, put it down," came the voice. And so on, for all three slides. The old chap was proud to do his bit for the hero of his Saturday afternoons!

'Not so very long ago, long after I myself had ceased examining, there was a curious incident at a Physiology examination written paper. The invigilator noticed that a quite unusual number of candidates asked leave to retire for a few minutes. He decided to investigate and found a textbook of physiology, bearing my name as part-author, in the lavatory! He had no idea who had consulted it and who had not, so the examination had to be scrapped and fresh papers prepared.'

Teacher of Surgery

Those who serve and contribute to the advancement of medical science can be briefly divided into three main groups. There are (i) those whose work lies on the advancing fringe of the new knowledge and who by research provide us continually with sharper tools; (ii) those who actually carry out the unremitting day-to-day practice of surgery in all its manifold branches and who become utterly engrossed in their ceaseless toil; and (iii) those who have a calling to instruct the next generation and who dedicate themselves to the duty of passing on the torch. It was the experience of A.R.S. to succeed in all three, but finally to find the highest fulfilment of his ability in undergraduate teaching. He was a first-rate teacher but he acquired his skill the hard way and in spite of the fact that he was submerged in practice. As a result, his teaching had this great advantage, that it was not merely theoretical. It had been hammered out in the school of practical experience. Illustrations are not hard to find. The *Lancet* commented at the time of his death – 'He was a general surgeon in the best sense of the word, and as a diagnostician he yielded place to none'.

The students, during the years when A.R.S. emerged as an outstanding teacher, regarded his prowess with some awe. He obviously was also advancing the development of surgery, and soon became something of a 'household' name. In a medical students' magazine, *The Stethoscope,* a writer, who calls himself Vertebra Prominens, addresses an adulatory 'Open letter to Mr. A. Rendle Short'. Amongst other things, he writes 'You have published a valuable little book *When to advise Operation in General Practice,* and have also written, amongst others, articles on "Surgical Work" and "Rectal Feeding". As a surgeon you are, perhaps, the most enterprising in Bristol. Given reasonable grounds, you do not hesitate to put into practice the most up-to-date surgical teaching, and are at present a keen disciple of Albee and his bone surgery. We feel sure that before long you will finally decide on some definite surgical cure for "Intestinal Stasis", even if it involves total enterectomy, and the establishment of a valvular opening into the portal vein through which suitably digested food can be administered. You have a wider knowledge than anyone we know of the rules and traditions of the Bristol Royal Infirmary, and are always delighted to impart your knowledge to students and residents alike.'

We have A.R.S.'s account of the early difficulties of a young surgeon. It throws much light on many aspects of a surgical career at that time. It must be remembered that these come from the days when all surgical appointments at the teaching hospitals carried no salary. The surgeons were totally dependent for their income on private cases sent to them by general practitioners.

'Although finding a place on the surgical staff of a hospital had not brought in any direct financial reward, it was always likely that doctors would begin to send their patients along for private consultations or operation. At any rate, it was so if they were assured that the young surgeon intended to play fair with them, and only took cases who came to him on the introduction of their own family practitioner. Patients often try to obtain a consultation without their doctor's knowledge and think it hard when this is refused. It is, however, better in the long run to have a firm rule and to observe it strictly. The young surgeon has much to learn about the right lines to follow in dealing both with doctors and with private patients, and not least, what fee to charge.

'One of the very first private operations I was invited to perform was for varicose veins, and the lady was sent me by one of my former students. He had just qualified and was doing a locum for a few weeks for a doctor at the other end of Bristol. He stipulated that the fee must be small and he would give the anaesthetic himself. We would do the operation at a nurse's house. I believe I undertook to do it for ten guineas or so. The woman had lately come from Burma. Things went moderately well, except that my student gave the anaesthetic very indifferently. In the middle of the operation the patient opened her eyes and said, "Oh, there is Dr. Brown!" During her convalescence, I heard that her husband poured out on her bed a handful of rubies, as "a present for being a good girl". I remember ruminating on the doleful fact that *one* of them would have bought my entire fortune at that time!

'Very shortly after that incident I was invited to operate on a hand case in a home across the Bristol Channel. Surgery in a private house means taking an enormous number of instruments and dressings that every hospital or nursing home normally provides. I was very concerned lest I should forget anything that mattered. However, all went well until we came to the very end, and then discovered that we had not brought a bandage! Some deficiencies can be concealed from the public eye, but not that. So I had to own up, and ask the doctor to run home in his car and fetch one. I well remember another case of this same practitioner's which also had to be operated on in a small private house, for appendix abscess. The father paid me my fee entirely in half-crowns, which weighed down my pockets heavily on the homeward journey. I suppose he distrusted banks and paper money!'

CHAPTER 8

Stories of a Surgeon

*There is only one rule of practice, put yourself in
the patient's place.*

Joseph Lister

All those students who were surgical 'dressers' for A.R.S. will remember teatime in the Surgeon's room at the Infirmary. It always followed the same routine. Tea was brought in by Wheeler, or Frank, with a few comments about the cricket or local gossip. Then the paper bags containing the sugared buns were put on the table and offered round. If there were not enough Wheeler was sent for more. And then hot, sweet tea, reviving and refreshing. A short pause till the first cup was gone and, then, amid drifts of conversation would come the invariable opening gambit (with its burr) 'I well remember . . . ' and for another fifteen minutes there followed story after story, always in the well-known accent and with the typical touches of humour. Many were instructive medically and all revealed the foibles of human nature. They also expressed his affection for his colleagues. Any of his former students reading the following pages may well imagine themselves back amid the sugared buns.

'For a long time men wounded in the 1914–18 war continued to come up for treatment. I well remember one such was a young fellow who walked into my out-patient room with both arms dropped straight by his sides, and announced that he could not move either of them. Someone had to open the door to let him in. There were scars of bullet-wounds and operations over the brachial plexus at the root of the neck of the right side, and he had in his pocket army documents to the effect that he had been discharged with gunshot wound of the brachial plexus causing irremediable paralysis of the arm. He had taken a job in Bristol as a lift-boy, but today had suddenly been seized with paralysis of the left arm.

'I pointed out to the students that this must obviously be a hysterical mimicry of the injured limb. I remember lifting his left arm over his head and then letting it drop; he brought it down quite slowly to hang by his side as before. I told him to come up the next day for some electrical treatment in the physio-therapy department. He went home, asked his landlady to give him his dinner with a spoon and fork as he could not feed himself and then to light a cigarette for him. While he sat and smoked it, he thought things over, and suddenly recovered the complete use of both arms. I confess I had barely looked at the right arm. I took it for granted, it being a very busy out-patient session with a lot of patients waiting, that the army forms were correct. What a godsend such a patient would have been to a faith-healing practitioner!'

Surgeon's Stories

A.R.S.'s anecdotes from the busy periods of his surgical career were of special value to the students. He would emphasise their significance with his dry humour in a way which made them live in the memories of these future practitioners. 'At times I have seen a number of cases with obvious self-inflicted injuries. A local practitioner, who was deputizing for the out-patient physician during the war, brought in a girl to see me who was in the habit of developing a rash on her face at mid-day every Wednesday. It cleared up in a few days afterwards. The distribution of the rash, on the cheeks and nose, corresponded to a skin disease called lupus erythematosus, but the appearance was quite different and was evidently due to some irritant. I admitted her to the wards one Wednesday morning and during the week the rash failed to appear. What made her choose Wednesday for her display we never discovered.

'Then there was a young woman who came up with a needle in her knee-joint. The knee was covered with operation scars and it was found that this was about the eleventh occasion on which she had pushed a needle in. We removed it and made her sign a paper, "I, Margaret . . . , promise that I will not put any more needles into my knee." When a man does himself a mischief the reason is usually plain enough. I was for a short time at a C.C.S. for self-inflicted wounds in France during the war; the men were trying to get sent back to England. When it is a woman the motives lie deep.

'A man was brought in one day with a foot so badly crushed that amputation was the only possible treatment. He had had a little alcohol. I explained the programme to him, and he agreed. He was sitting up on the operating table. "Lie down", I said, "and we will give you an anaesthetic." "I don't want any anaesthetic", said he. I told him that was absurd; of course he must have an anaesthetic. It would be too painful otherwise. "I won't have it. I can stick it", he replied. He looked just like Captain Kettle, with bright eyes, a little black beard trimmed to a point, folded arms, sitting there on the table. I re-opened the argument. "I tell you, I won't have any anaesthetic", he repeated. "Take it off. If you knew your business it would be off by now." That decided it. I cut the flaps without another word and was just starting to saw through the bone when he lay back on the table and said, "I'll have some." Nowadays, of course, we would have given him a spinal, or even a local, anaesthetic.

'One day a Bristol doctor, Dr. Lavington, who often entrusted me with his surgical cases, rang up to ask me to call at his house to see a patient with a strangulated hernia who had just come to consult him. I went, and advised immediate removal to a nursing home for operation. As this was being discussed sounds of loud lamentations arose in the entrance hall outside. We looked out, and there was a man of about sixty, a near neighbour, in the deepest distress. "Oh, doctor," he cried, "my sister has cut her throat. Oh dear, oh dear, what shall I do? Come at once, come at once." He went down on his knees and sobbed bitterly. I asked where he lived. Lavington and I decided that he had better go to see the suicide, while I completed arrangements about the strangulated hernia and then I would come too.

'I called a taxi, got my patient away in it, and then went to the house of the tragedy. The brother seemed too upset to move from the doctor's entrance hall. I went up the garden path, and found the front door wide open. All was quiet. I went in. No one in sight. I shouted up the stairs, "Lavington, Lavington." No reply, I looked into the drawing-room and the dining-room; no one there. I did not like the business at all and went out into the street again to think about it. I was relieved to see Lavington coming along with two constables whom he had collected from the police station not far away. We went in again, looked once more into the ground-floor rooms, then in the basement. All was quiet and tidy; no one there. So we formed a little procession to mount the stairs.

The doctor went first, then the policemen, each holding his helmet in his hand; I brought up the rear. We looked fearfully at the bottom of the bedroom door, half expecting to see blood trickling out.

'Suddenly the door burst open and a very flushed and angry lady, partly dressed, who had evidently been lying down for an afternoon siesta, exclaimed indignantly, "Doctor Lavington. What are you doing in my house? And the police, too! How dare you?" The doctor very hesitatingly and apologetically explained that he had had a message to say she had cut her throat. "Nothing of the kind," she cried with great energy. "Get out of my house at once." We beat a very hasty retreat. "Lor, sir, wasn't she angry?" said a hot and bothered constable to me. We went back to the brother. He was still sobbing and lamenting in the hall. Of course, he was completely off his head, and had imagined the whole thing.

'On another occasion a doctor took me to see the proprietress of a very flourishing public house in a very squalid neighbourhood. She was stout and elderly, and had a strangulated umbilical hernia, which at her age and with her physique may be a very serious condition. We came downstairs and told the middle-aged man and the young woman who seemed to be in charge that there would have to be an operation, but that the prospects of success were not good. They both threw up their hands in dismay and cried, "But doctor, she hasn't made her will!" I was rather surprised, but gave them a couple of hours to get in a lawyer for the purpose. I asked the doctor why all this excitement. "Well," he explained, "the pub belonged to her first husband and there are two sons somewhere at the other end of England. This man is her second husband, and the young woman is no relation at all, but she has been looking after the old lady very assiduously. If she dies it all goes to the sons." The old lady made a will; but she also made a triumphant recovery.

Some Embarrassing Moments

'One of my first private house operations away from Bristol was in another Cathedral city. My equipment in those days was not as adequate as it became later and the doctor said that he would ask the local cottage hospital to send over a few things. As I was making my preparations, I heard a great racket on the stairs. The doctor stepped out and I heard him say, "Oh my lord, but we didn't wish to trouble you." To my astonishment there appeared just outside the door the bishop, complete with apron and gaiters, lugging in a heavy operating table. We thanked him, and he retired. I asked the doctor why his episcopal reverence should act as theatre porter. "Well, you see", said he, "he was visiting in the hospital at the time, and the bishop being a very gallant man, and nurse", casting an eye to see that she was listening, "and nurse being a very pretty woman, he insisted on helping the table along himself!"

'Another early experience was at a large country mansion not far from Bristol. The local doctor asked me to come to operate on the squire and to bring an anaesthetist. For some reason that I cannot remember, I was not given an opportunity of seeing the patient beforehand, which seemed odd. When the anaesthetist and I drove up to the house we noticed two or three cars at the door, which we assumed might belong to sympathetic relations. A footman answered our ring and took us upstairs to the bedroom. At the top of the stairs a lady stepped out of a room on the landing, looked at us in a constrained way and said would we mind waiting in the entrance hall. We did so. The walls were hung with trophies of the chase, and there was a lunch laid out for three. This, no doubt, was to be a first instalment of our reward.

Presently down came the bailiff of the estate, looking like a man who had a difficult duty to perform, to beg our pardon and to explain. It seems that the squire had a doctor in London, as well as in Bristol, and if he had to have an operation the London doctor laid down the law that no one must do it but our senior surgeon, Mr. Carwardine, and that Mr. Flemming must give the anaesthetic. As a matter of fact they were in the bedroom at the moment and the operation was well under way. He could not explain why we had not been notified of the change of plan. There was nothing for it but to go home again. When I got to my house there was an express letter from the doctor to announce the change of surgeons; he said he was too much ashamed to telephone, so was writing instead. I have often thought what a pity it was that the footman did not actually show us into the bedroom. I should have loved to have seen Flemming's face and heard his comments.

'Patients differ extraordinarily in their reaction, both physical and psychological, to serious injuries or operation that leave them temporarily or permanently crippled in one way or another. Of all those who have been under my own care the bravest and most successful in overcoming his disability was a master builder, over seventy years of age. It became necessary to amputate both his legs above the knee, with only a few months between these severe operations. I never dreamt that he would get about again. But the determined old boy had a pair of artificial legs made to his own specification, learned to walk with crutches, drove a car, and went around the scaffolding of buildings his firm were erecting, on a tour of inspection, in a wheel-barrow. I am told that when he came up the aisle of the church where he worshipped, members of the congregation were much affected. As 31st December drew near, his sons said to me, "Doctor, if you want a thrill, let the governor drive you round the town in his car. But it will have to be before the end of the year because none of the insurance companies will take him on again." '

Hospital Colleagues

Amongst his papers, A.R.S. left numerous interesting, and sometimes humorous, comments on his colleagues on the staff of the Royal Infirmary and the Medical Faculty of the University. Some are of interest here.

'Of all his colleagues, the one into whose company a surgeon, who is in private practice, is likely to be thrown most frequently is his anaesthetist. Year in year out, night and day, near and far, they work together. They probably like and respect each other because theirs is a voluntary association.* The surgeon could usually choose someone else. I was fortunate indeed that during the greater part of my active surgical life I was able to choose A. L. Flemming.

'He was painstaking to a degree, and almost hyperconscientious. On one occasion he had given open ether to a boy with acute appendicitis at Clifton College Sanatorium. All went well and I hurried off to a consultation. But the boy seemed a little dusky and Flemming sat with him an hour or two to be on the safe side. Next day he was very ill, temperature 104°, very blue, and the right lung completely dull with no air-entry. Flemming had to go to London by the morning train to attend a meeting of the Society of Anaesthetists. On the way he meditated gloomily about the boy and tried to think how it was that things had gone wrong. Suddenly he recollected seeing on the locker at the bedside, before the operation, some grape skins. That must be the explanation. No doubt the boy had eaten a surreptitious grape, skin and all. He had

---

* N.B. This was before the National Health Service was introduced.

regurgitated this skin, and it had been inhaled into the air passages. That would be the cause of the blocked air entry, the blueness, the fever. The next thing to happen would be an abscess of the lung, a long illness, a hazardous operation to drain, very likely lifelong invalidism. And – whose fault?

'It was a very apprehensive man who came across the road to see me late that night to propound his unhappy theory and gloomy prognostications. I was far from convinced about the inhaled grape skin; there had been no coughing during the induction. The following morning we found the temperature normal, the lung cleared up, and a measles rash in full bloom all over his face. The explanation was now clear. The boy had been unlucky enough to run into measles and appendicitis simultaneously and the ether had stirred up the preliminary measles catarrh into a transient pneumonia. Uneventful recovery followed.

'No doubt the two men on the staff of the Bristol hospitals in my time, who would be best known to the medical world elsewhere, were Carey Coombs and Hey Groves. Coombs was a really scientific physician. He did pioneer work on rheumatic nodules in heart-muscle and became a leading authority on rheumatic heart disease. It is tragic that he should have died himself of cardiac disease, at a comparatively early age. There has never been such a crowded congregation at a medical funeral in Bristol as on the occasion when Carey Coombs was laid to rest.

'Hey Groves* the orthopaedic surgeon, had a very difficult time when he was a student. It was a constant struggle between enthusiasm, poverty and frustration. Surgery always attracted him, and he used to take patients into his own house to operate on them, or alternatively, he did operations in their homes. His appointment to the staff of the Bristol General Hospital took place while I was a resident and it did not take us long to discover that a fresh breeze was blowing over those somewhat stagnant waters. He introduced spinal anaesthesia; he cut the posterior spinal nerve-roots to relieve tonic spasm in paralysed people; he was the first to remove the Gasserian ganglion for intractable neuralgia. Later he took up bone and joint surgery as a specialism.

'He was a member of the little group of pioneers, under the leadership of Sir Robert Jones, who more or less gave up general

* Hey Groves was brought up in the same religious community as Rendle Short. He was grandson of Antony Norris Groves, a pioneeer in the earliest of missions of the Christian Brethren.

surgery to devote themselves to orthopaedic surgery in the widened sense of the word. Here he found abundant scope for his enormous enterprise and his mechanical skill. He was an expert carpenter, and constantly invented new methods of carpentering bones. Surgeons used to come from all over the world to watch Hey Groves at work. The numerous gun-shot fractures of the war of 1914–18 furnished him with plentiful material, but it was disappointing material on account of lurking sepsis. Months after a wound had healed and all seemed quiet, any attempt at surgery would bring about an acute flare-up, and many a piece of splendid carpentering was ruined in consequence. If only he could have had penicillin to hold sepsis in check! He was constantly experimenting with daring methods of bone-grafting. Perhaps the most remarkable was the case in which he built up a new humerus for a lad with repeated beef-bone grafts, and the patient eventually, as an undergraduate, won the putting-the-weight event for his university with the beef-bone arm.

'It was not only in devising and carrying out new operations that Hey Groves showed his enterprise. He started the *British Journal of Surgery* and succeeded in forming a Bristol and Bath Surgeon's Club to visit other clinics throughout the country. He also set a fashion for teams of British surgeons to visit famous clinics overseas. He was my predecessor in the Chair of Surgery in the University of Bristol. He was a brilliant lecturer to doctors and surgeons, not so good to students, though he wrote a very popular *Synopsis of Surgery* for their use. His latter years were clouded. He had a stroke which crippled all his activities sadly.'

Loyalty to Colleagues

A.R.S. never missed an opportunity of paying tribute to the doctors in general practice who were in the habit of entrusting him with their surgical cases.

'For a professional man to feel that people constantly look to him for advice is bound to have an effect on his character, and it is a serious temptation to him to become opinionated and pontifical. Personal mannerisms are likely to become more pronounced. The more he is isolated from his professional brethren, the greater the danger. He tends to become wise in his own conceit. To mix with others, to hear his diagnosis and treatment reviewed by someone else equally competent, and to have his confident opinion brought to the test of the operating table or the post-mortem room:

these are the safeguards. "I beg you, gentlemen, to conceive it possible that you may be mistaken" would be, for some, a very good motto. But, pushed too far, it is ruinous. The doctor who is constantly distrustful of his own opinion, or is afraid to form one, inspires no confidence and has a miserable life.'

It was a constant trait that A.R.S. never grumbled about his colleagues behind their backs. Shortly after his death a colleague paid tribute to this fact. At the Bristol Medical Chirurgical Society Meeting in October 1953 the President, Dr. G. E. F. Sutton, remarked 'The absence of Professor Rendle Short remains a silent gap with all of us. He was a man who never thought ill of others. I remember when I first got to know him how I found him gruff and sometimes very off-hand in manner; but when I got to know him better I realized how genuine and real was his whole personality. I recollect that in a committee room where a certain member was being criticized and castigated by everybody, Mr. Short remained silent until the end, when he said that, as we had not got the prisoner here it was impossible to put him in the box in order to permit him to make his reply. "Moreover", he said, "none of us really is in a position to cast stones at him. If our criticisms of him are true, which I more than doubt, we ought not to talk about it in his absence. Indeed, perhaps it may not be true, and I sincerely hope not." Having said this he left the committee.'

Similar evidence of his strict integrity was apparent in matters which concerned his personal affairs and professional advancement. At a vital point in his early career, the most influential man on an appointments board suggested to A.R.S. a somewhat dubious course of action. In return he was promised the man's full backing which would virtually have ensured that the job would be his. The reply was: 'I cannot do it, because both modesty and my Christian faith forbid me to do so.'

CHAPTER 9

The Professor of Surgery

Your profession offers the most complete and constant union of those three qualities which have the greatest charm for pure and active minds – novelty, utility, charity.
James Paget

The full extent of A.R.S.'s ability and prodigious industry was not recognised at its fullest until his appointment as Professor of Surgery in the University of Bristol in 1933. He was already known as an excellent teacher in the fundamentals of Surgery and Physiology. He had written numerous papers and written or helped to edit several books. As Professor, he now more and more became an 'institution' at the Infirmary. Few of the teaching staff were giving as much systematic instruction or were as useful to the average clinical medical student who was approaching his final examination. This was outstandingly true of A.R.S.'s flair for diagnosis and, particularly, for differential diagnosis. As one of the senior medical staff commented to a friend at the time – 'If I had to fall into the hands of the surgeons, then, however prominent they were, so long as Rendle Short could be brought in to determine *what was wrong* and *what had to be done* – I wouldn't mind about the rest and who it was who actually did it!' This was a well deserved tribute to the diagnostic accuracy and sound judgment of the new Professor.

Publications

Among A.R.S.'s more academic contributions to Surgery in a wider setting were (i) his editorship of *The Index of Prognosis* and co-editorship (for thirty-four years) of *The Medical Annual*, and (ii) his work as an undergraduate teacher. His pen was always busy, but it certainly worked to no mean purpose in the case of these two monumental undertakings, which carried his name far beyond Bristol. *The Index of Prognosis,* first published in 1915, was one of the four massive reference volumes* undertaken by John Wright & Son of Bristol in order to supply the busy practitioner with up-to-date sources of quick reference on conditions which were likely to confront them. It was the first attempt of the kind to bring together what was known in a difficult and neglected branch of medicine. A.R.S.'s previous investigations into 'end results' of disease made him specially aware of the data in this field. The task of keeping up-to-date for subsequent editions must not only have been exacting, but have demanded a large proportion of his time.

At a later stage an even more testing task must have been the production each year of the surgical sections in *The Medical Annual,* which was a summary of references to, and descriptions of, all work of importance in medical research of that year. He was fortunate in sharing the work with gifted, well-organized, and industrious colleagues. Such an undertaking entailed hours of correspondence, assessments and then writing up the vast amount of material obtained. As *The Lancet* commented 'Industry and superb organization enabled him to put twice the amount of useful work into the day than most can manage.'

The purely surgical problem which A.R.S. investigated most thoroughly was the etiology of appendicitis. He had written an article on this subject in 1920 in the *British Journal of Surgery* and in 1946, twenty-five years later, produced a book entitled *The Causation of Appendicitis* reviewing the subject in the light of further research. He put forward the theory that lack of cellulose in the diet was the main factor in its causation. For this purpose he surveyed figures of the national distribution of appendicitis and dietary habits of most of the nations of the world. He collected data from many sources and draws on his own considerable experience in his assessment of the evidence.†

Skill as a Teacher

Hippocrates taught that in Medicine or Surgery it is par-

---

* The companion volumes were *The Index of Symptoms* (H. Letheby Tidy), *The Index of Differential Diagnosis of Main Symptoms* (Herbert French) and *The Index of Treatment* (Robert Hutchinson).

† The subject has received recent further attention in the work of D. P. Burkitt and Surg. Capt. T. L. Cleave.

ticularly important that a student pay due reverence to his teacher. But this respect is not easily engendered unless the teacher's skill as an instructor convince the student of his competence and knowledge. Judged by the high esteem in which his former pupils held him, A.R.S. was a teacher in the highest class. There was nothing he enjoyed more than the informal teaching by the bedside, which he carried through with ease and clarity. Also, he revelled in the give and take of his 'grinds'.* For these sessions, usually held in the Museum of Pathology, he used the Socratic method of 'question and answer'. In an open letter to him in *The Stethoscope* the students wrote: 'Whether you are lecturing in Physiology or demonstrating in Surgery you have a style all your own – an extraordinary lucidity without padding, and one feels in taking down your lectures almost word for word that some "notes" at any rate are going to be of use in the future.'

His successor in the Chair of Surgery – Professor Milnes-Walker – wrote in the *British Journal of Surgery:* 'Undoubtedly his greatest asset to the Bristol Medical School was his undergraduate teaching at which he was a master. The older of his past students remember him first in the Department of Physiology, where his outstanding lectures on the central nervous system demonstrated that a most difficult subject could be presented in a manner which all could understand and retain. His clinical teaching was of the same order – clear, incisive, dogmatic; with complete absorption in the task of the moment, he would pick out the salient points in each case and drive them home. He was best on the well-known conditions of every day and would bring in some of his funny anecdotes whenever possible always starting with "I well remember". Among his most attractive traits was his sense of humour which crept into almost all his teaching and there must be many who will never forget his apposite similes. "The tonsils always remind me of a pair of 'chuckers out' at a place of popular entertainment. They stand, one on each side of the door to deal with any rowdy customers that may come along. It is easy to understand that if the 'chuckers out' be old and stout they get the worst of the encounter." This, with a twinkle in his eye, for it is doubtful if he ever went to a place of popular entertainment and

---

* 'Grinds', in the student slang of the day, were sessions where the question and answer method – in Socratic style – was used to 'grind' the students' minds into shape, being followed by a brief summary of what should have been said by the students.

certainly not one of the variety which necessitated the employment of "chuckers out".

'On Mondays at noon he gathered the final year students around him and by question and answer and oft quoted aphorisms would awaken interest in the most lethargic minds. He knew all the students by name and could usually give a fair outline of their background and followed them keenly throughout their careers. When he knew that one of them was in pecuniary difficulties he would, if they had any aptitude, ask them out to assist in private for which he gave them immediately afterwards the sum of one guinea, usually paid as one pound note, one sixpence and six coppers.

'All his lectures on diseases were memorized and classified. His Bristol accent, which was riper in earlier years, called forth the following erudition in the medical students' magazine of the day:

"There was a great surgeon called Short
Who classified all that he tort.
  His classification
  Embraced all creation
For he tort all he thort that he ort." '

Students' Stories

The similes, aphorisms and anecdotes which accompanied his teaching rounds and 'grinds' are easily recoverable wherever one meets one of his former students. Any former member of the Bristol Medical School who may chance to read these lines will remember the effective Bristol accent which was often purposely accentuated to rub in a lesson. 'On one occasion our Physiology class arrived to find on the desk of the Physiology lecture theatre a viper, killed on the Mendips by a man named Cooper, who brought it as a votive offering to "the Chief". On the latter's arrival he was delighted, and lifting the prey up before the class exclaimed "Coopurrr here has caught a vipurrr! My word, Coopurrr, what a rippurrr!" '

On one occasion he had asked a student the pathology of acholuric jaundice. The student, who thought himself quite an expert in pathology, talked for quite a time on the symptomatology, etiology, and pathology of the condition. Eventually A.R.S., to emphasize his point, said 'Yes, yes, that may be. But what I say is that this spleen *dislikes, distrusts,* and *devours* those blood corpuscles!' He was very keen on accurate spelling and, on reading a dresser's mis-spelt notes one day, remarked acidly: ' "Vomitting" is only spelt with two t's when it is especially severe!'

To a student who was inclined to answer without adequate reflection A.R.S. asked: 'The charwoman from the B.R.I. has knelt on a rusty nail and it has punctured the knee-joint. What would you do?' *Student:* 'I would wash out the wound with Eusol.' *A.R.S.:* 'Anything else?' *Student:* 'No'. *A.R.S.* 'Right. Having lost that leg for her, what would you do next?'(!). To another student who, on being questioned concerning the dosage of a certain treatment, gave the answer in ounces when she meant drachms, he commented drily: 'And what would you do then? Square the coroner or flee the country?'

Some Typical Aphorisms

All his teaching, classifications and mnemonics were spiced with a robust common sense which quickly communicated itself to the students. They learnt to approach Surgery in the right manner and to differentiate the wood from the trees. Each ward-round, each session in out-patients, and each 'grind' in the Pathological Museum was likely to yield the note-taking student a new collection of 'gems' of which the following are just a few general examples:

1. (In examinations, or in the consulting room.) 'Diagnose the *common* things and in 99 per cent of the cases you will be right!'
2. 'Think of the *simplest* thing it might be and you will often at once be near the mark. Then, think of the *worst* thing it might be, in order to exclude the worst emergency. Then run over in your mind the things in between.'
3. 'Don't tell the examiner more than he asks; he may make you pay for it!'
4. (In getting into right perspective the 'stocking anaesthesia' and functional paralysis of a limb in a case of hysteria). 'The point is: "She says, 'I *cannot*'; her friends say, 'She *will* not'; the truth is that she *cannot will*" '.

Teaching for him was not a necessary, but unprofitable, duty attached to his post in a teaching hospital. It was part of his life and he entered into it with enthusiastic ability. His rounds were always well attended by a full quota of students who appreciated his powers of communication and his humour, and responded to his sallies.

A.R.S. would frequently speak of the difficult decisions which would confront the students in the days ahead. Most of the surgeon's problems relate to the difficulties in complicated circumstances of making an accurate diagnosis, choosing the appropriate treatment, and deciding concerning the right time to operate. New remedies and new methods are continually being developed and it may be difficult to know whether or not the new is any improvement on the old. These, however, are only the technical matters. There are also a number of surgical dilemmas in which the point at issue is important to all concerned, and everyone has a right to arrive at an informed opinion. The following are some of his hints to students.

Obtaining Consent for Operation

'There is often the question of obtaining permission for an operation. In ordinary cases, of course, this is quite simple; the nature of the treatment proposed is explained, and an adult patient either does, or does not, consent. If the patient is a minor, no operation ought to be performed unless permission is granted by a parent or guardian. It is always wise for the surgeon to have the permission put into writing, and in many hospitals this is the rule. So far so good; but in practice, things are not always so simple. When I was a house-surgeon a maid-servant aged twenty was admitted to hospital with a perforated gastric ulcer. In such cases the perforation has to be closed by operation with all speed; if this is done under twelve hours they mostly recover; if over twenty-four hours, they nearly all die.* I rang up the consultant surgeon and he came to see her. She lived at a village twenty miles away. It was a Saturday evening. She was quite willing to be operated on but there was no way of getting into touch with the parents, though a telegram was sent. The surgeon, strictly obeying the law of the land, refused to operate until permission arrived. On Monday morning it came. He operated, but she died. In my judgment he was legally right, but morally wrong. The proper line to take would have been to call in a colleague to give a second opinion, and if he agreed, to operate. Surely the law would have condoned such a decision?

'One evening a public schoolboy was sent in to the school sanatorium with symptoms of acute appendicitis, but the pain was

* In recent years developments in modern treatment have considerably altered the outlook for the better.

not severe, and the pulse and temperature were normal. We rang up the parents, who lived in a remote village in the Home Counties, and explained that an operation would be necessary if the symptoms got worse, and might we take it that they gave permission? The answer was that we should in that case ring back again and ask. With this we had to be content. The symptoms did get worse. By eleven o'clock the pain was severe and the pulse and temperature rising. We put through another call. No reply, in spite of repeated rings. We asked the telephone exchange to ring the house next door. Apparently there was no house near. Then could they send a messenger? No, there was no one available. Eventually they rang the nearest police station and a constable went on his bicycle and knocked the family up, with great difficulty, at 2 a.m. They had all gone to sleep and slept soundly. By the time that the telephoned permission came through we were pretty tired of waiting for it, especially the patient, whose pain had become intolerable. On the first day of the following term the boy's mother walked into my consulting room with her younger son, a new boy. "If this one gets appendicitis," she said, "operate first and ask afterwards."

'It is not as a rule difficult to obtain consent, if the surgeon firmly believes that it is his duty in the patient's interest to press for it. But old folk living in the country, and especially farmers, are sometimes obdurate. I was taken to a remote farmhouse in Somerset to see a man of about fifty-five with appendicitis. It was on the second or third day of the illness. We thought the appendix was just about to perforate, or had just perforated. At this point in the development of the condition, owing to the relief of tension in the appendix, there is often a deceptive lull in the pain. It is sometimes called the "fool's paradise" stage, and it was just at this time that we called on farmer "X". We did our best to persuade him to have the appendix removed, to avert the danger of widespread peritonitis. He was adamant. Probably it was dislike of leaving home that influenced him most. We talked to the wife and son and they added their appeals to ours, but in vain.

'After quite a long time spent in arguments and coaxing we gave it up and drove away. Just after the car started the farmer changed his mind and sent his son to tell us so; but he had no car and we were now out of sight. There was no telephone. So, quite ignorant of the changed situation, I went back to Bristol. Next day I was sent for in a hurry. General peritonitis was now established.

He put up a good fight and lived a week. Probably modern methods in a good nursing home or hospital would have saved him, and no doubt at all removal of the appendix on the previous day would have done so. But such cases of obstinacy are, in my experience, rare. It used to be far otherwise. Sir Frederick Treves tells how in his young days he tried to persuade a woman to allow her daughter to be operated on, and got the reply, "That's all right, young man, but who is going to pay for the funeral?"

'It does not do, however, to assure patients that they will die if they refuse an operation. I had an early lesson in this matter. An old lady, with what I thought was an intestinal obstruction, declined surgical treatment in spite of my assuring her that she would die, if she did not have an operation. She vowed that she had been like this before, but that she always got well on the third day. "If I'm not better tomorrow, you shall operate, but I won't have anything done today." I argued, but all in vain. She *did* get well on the third day. Probably she had a low opinion of surgeons for the rest of her life, and I have avoided a cocksure statement ever since!

When, or not, to Operate

'The question of operation or no operation has sometimes to be decided not on medical grounds, but on a consideration of all the circumstances. There was never a wiser piece of advice than this: "the doctor's business is to treat *the patient,* not the disease". The patient may be old, or insane, or for some reason or another his life may be of no value to himself or anybody else. Or, the condition may be hopeless. Hopeless patients are sometimes only too eager to be operated upon.'

'Elderly folk stand operations, under modern conditions, better than might be expected. I have done quite considerable life-saving operations with success on patients over ninety. Whether it is wise or kind to prolong their lives by heroic surgery is another matter; each case must be taken on its merits. The main consideration is whether the patient is suffering pain or distress. I have always advised operation, at any age, to relieve pain or distress. But to operate on an octogenarian merely to prolong life is quite often wrong treatment, in my judgment.

'Much the same considerations should guide the surgeon who is invited to operate on a patient certified as insane or feeble-minded. It is only common humanity to do all that is possible to relieve pain or distress. No one in his senses would want to prolong the life of a patient who is a chronic dement. Some patients, however, who are technically classified as feeble-minded can do very useful work of a routine character and quite enjoy their limited lives. They are certainly entitled to whatever benefit surgical treatment can bring them.

Communicating Bad News

'One of the most difficult and painful tasks that must be performed by the surgeon, or for that matter by any doctor, is to decide how much of bad news should be imparted to the patient, or to his friends, and the method of telling. It is usually advised, in hopeless cases, to tell the relatives everything and the patient nothing. In a general way there is much to be said for this course. But it is very wrong to adopt a hard and fast rule. It saves a good deal of trouble, and relieves the doctor from a lot of thinking, to stick to the rule. But that is bad doctoring. For instance, patients are not always on good terms with their relatives and might hate the idea that a relative should be given priority of information. Relatives are sometimes fools, not fit to be trusted with important business.

'The common dilemma is to decide what to say to the patient himself, and how to say it. I had two early lessons on this difficult subject. One was a farmer with advanced cancer of the stomach, who came up to see me without any relatives, from a village in Somerset. When he heard from me that the outlook was serious, he went straight to bed, made no more effort to see to things, and gave up all for lost. The other case was that of an old lady with a recurrent sarcoma following amputation. She asked me flat out how long she had to live. Foolishly I said, "Less than a year, I am afraid." She burst into tears. If I had said, "Only a few weeks" she would have rejoiced. She dreaded life, not death.

'Fortunately, in my experience, not one patient in ten who is gravely ill asks for any information. Often, no doubt, they suspect that things are serious but prefer that it should not be put into words. Sometimes it is wise not to wait for any questions but to anticipate them by rushing in with quite a lot of information which nevertheless evades the main point. One can at least plan beforehand just what to say and what not to say.

'In general, no doubt, it is wiser and kinder to tell the patient who is not likely to recover as little as possible; but to this rule there are some important exceptions. One is, when he is minded to lay out a lot of money on schemes from which he will not live to reap any benefit. Not long ago, in America, a wealthy man brought an action against his doctor for not telling him he had a mortal disease, with the result that he had invested a large sum of money which was from his point of view completely lost. He would probably have won his action, which would have created a very awkward legal precedent, but he died before the case was heard in the courts. Again, some patients become exceedingly dissatisfied with their doctor because they do not improve under his treatment, and it may be necessary to disillusion them. I have known patients very angry with their relatives or doctor for making light of a dangerous illness; it had seemed to them heartless and lacking in sympathy. On one occasion, a husband found himself cut out of his wife's will because he told her there was nothing seriously the matter when she knew that she was dying.

'A few doctors, and a good many relatives and nurses, save themselves the trouble of thinking out what is the wisest and kindest thing to tell the patient in that particular case, by restoring to what they call "white lies". This is to be deprecated. There is, of course, for many of us a moral question involved. We do not in the least feel compelled to blurt out the whole unpleasant truth to everybody but we do recognize that it can never be right to tell downright, deliberate lies. But quite apart from the moral issue, it is not even good tactics. It would be most unfortunate if the general public got into its head that doctors are in the habit of telling their patients deliberate lies. You can only lie once. Any man can deceive me once, and easily; but having been deceived once I shall never believe another word he says. Confidence is wrecked. Is it helpful to a dying person to know, or suspect, that no one is playing straight with him? He prefers to feel that the doctor, at least, can be trusted. Granted that it requires thought, and insight, and sympathy, to say the right thing, at the right time, and that every case needs different handling, nevertheless the effort ought to be made.'

Euthanasia

'There is much difference of opinion, as to the justifiability of euthanasia, that is to say, of giving a lethal dose of a narcotic or similar drug to people who are supposed to be hopelessly ill, and in great suffering. Many argue quite hotly on the subject. It is one of those circumstances where sentiment clamours against judgment.

Here, again, there is a moral issue involved. Many of us remember that it has been said, "Thou shalt not kill" and that is final and sufficient. But, without falling back on that prohibition, or invoking the law of the land, which could of course be changed, let us consider the matter dispassionately. Doctors have no liking for the rôle of Lord High Executioner. We think that euthanasia is quite definitely wrong.

'Some people say, however, that it may be justified when three clearly proved facts are present: (i) the patient cannot recover; (ii) his pain is not going to get better even under treatment; (iii) and he steadfastly desires to die, i.e. it is not a mere passing fit of despair. The relatives may be tired of looking after him but that reason is totally inadequate. Now, so many surprising things happen in Medicine and Surgery that the experienced doctor can very seldom be quite sure of these three things, and if he is not sure, the question does not arise. As the law stands at present a million patients are sure, and rightly so, that the doctor is trying to cure them or relieve them and that he will not willingly poison them. If once that assurance is removed for the sake of a tiny handful of hopeless cases, all the million will lose confidence. The doctor-patient relationship is altered. An unselfish woman, gravely ill, who dreads poison and death but feels that she is a burden on her family, would pretend to want to die, for their sakes. The conscience of the civilized world was shocked when the Nazis put out of the way their aged, insane and unwanted persons, and the conscience of the world was right. There are usually ways round the difficulty.

'Mind Cures' and 'Faith Healing'

'The alleged cures after the ministrations of Christian Scientists or faith-healing missions are by no means always permanent or even long-lasting, and they fall almost always into one of the following categories. Perhaps the patient was a chronic invalid, liable to ups and downs, and only too anxious to convince himself that he was better. Or, a patient who had been making the worst of an ailment decided to make the best of it. Or, there had been a medical mistake as to the diagnosis. Or, the condition was "functional", and the excitement of a big meeting highly charged with emotion, or the promises of an enthusiastic healer, effected a sudden cure. That is to say, nearly all the cases can be simply explained by "suggestion".

'Practitioners of faith-healing who tell those who come to

them that it shows lack of trust in God to take medicines or to accept the services of a doctor, or who give a firm promise that they will be cured, go beyond the Scriptures, and may do great harm. Patients who derive no benefit, or who later relapse, may suffer a serious eclipse of faith concerning things spiritual as well as temporal. In one case a young woman, suffering from pulmonary tuberculosis, who had been under the care of a medical relative of mine and for whom a bed at a sanatorium had been reserved, went to a faith-healing mission. She thought that she had been cured, and refused the bed. Months later, when she was much worse, she requested admission. But how many of her relatives had she infected in the interval? A friend has told me of a faith-healing mission which sent fifty of its workers to a malarious region of Africa, all of them under the conviction that it was wrong to take quinine. In two years every one of them was either dead or had left the field.

'My own experience of Christian Science patients and practitioners has been small, but interesting. On one occasion the leading Christian Science practitioner in a certain town sent for me in a hurry, because she thought her companion had dislocated her shoulder. On another occasion, after I had seen a man in consultation and told relatives that nothing could be done, his wife, a leading Christian Science practitioner, called on me to ask me not to let her views influence my decision (whatever that might mean). I was once summoned urgently to a house used by the Christian Scientists as a kind of hospital to see an unfortunate woman, who had an advanced, ulcerating, very painful cancer of the breast. No dressings and no sedatives had been supplied for her, and the stench and filth were appalling. It was far too late to save her life, but it was possible to relieve her last few weeks. Christian Science is seen at its cruellest when children, after a serious injury, or in pain, are given nothing but a chapter from Mrs. Eddy's book.

'The Bible does not support the theory that it is wrong to take medicines, or wrong to consult a physician. To say so is to draw a quite illogical distinction between food, which is a gift of God, and efficacious medicines, which are also a gift of God. It is true that Asa was reproved for turning not to the Lord but to the physicians when he was suffering from a long-lasting and painful disease, but they may very well have been foreign and pagan practitioners. It is true that there is no mention of physicians in the Epistle of James, but we may be sure that the number of Christian physicians available was very limited and local, and some of the others, at least, would use heathen remedies. Paul told Timothy to take 'wine for his stomach's sake, and his often infirmities'. Christ would, we may well think, scarcely speak of the Good Samaritan pouring in oil and wine as a treatment for wounds, if He did not wish His followers to take similar action. Nor would He have said, "They that are whole have no need of a physician, but they that are sick" if He meant that His disciples must not send for a physician.'

Illustrations of the robust common sense and practicality of Rendle Short's whole outlook could be multiplied. The medical students and postgraduates gained from their Professor of Surgery not only a sound training in diagnosis and treatment, but also gentle wisdom in coping with human nature during the course of their professional lives. They also received stimulus to keep their eyes open and to seek to add to relevant knowledge and research.

CHAPTER 10

Servant of Christ

*The law of truth was in his mouth, and iniquity
was not found in his lips; he walked with me in
peace and equity, and did turn many away from
iniquity.*

Malachi 2:6

There can be no doubt that the basic motivation and interest of A.R.S. was spiritual. Strong as were his loyalties and service to the medical profession and the city of Bristol, he was in the first place an ardent disciple of Christ. Truth, as he saw it, was grounded in spiritual realities. Christ had affirmed 'I am the way, the truth and the life' and he wholeheartedly accepted that claim, But it was precisely because of this that he so energetically gave his mind to the pursuit of medical progress and the task of spreading its benefits to the developing countries overseas.

Today there is widespread misunderstanding of the place of religion in relation to intellectual progress. It is often inaccurately implied that scientific research and social advance have been inhibited by any great devotion to a religion. On the contrary, both Judaism and the Christian faith can claim that the exact opposite has been the case. For many of their best minds have pursued science with distinction, regarding it as their allotted task in serving the one true God. It was such a clear conviction, associated with his ruthless logic, which moulded the life of A.R.S. There was no double mind.

In this respect, and in a genius coming from a very similar religious background, the closest parallel amongst scientists is to be found in the life of Michael Faraday (1791–1867). The latter was brought up in the London congregation of the Sandemanians (or Glassites), a small Presbyterian sect originating from the Scottish Lowlands. Throughout his life Faraday remained a devoted and active member of this community. He would return over the week-end during any meeting of the British Association in a provincial city in order not to be absent from their Sunday worship. In one of Faraday's earliest biographies the story is told how that at the close of one of his public lectures, when the Prince Consort and a large number of scientists and prominent people had gathered to do him honour, he was given a standing ovation. When the cheers and clapping had ceased the audience waited for a reply. The rostrum had been vacated. The lecturer had unobtrusively slipped through the door behind the desk and was on his way to the most important event in his week, the prayer meeting at the Sandemanian chapel! A.R.S. similarly made every endeavour not to be prevented from attending Bethesda on a Monday or the Shaftesbury Crusade on a Thursday night. For, as Christ declared, 'Where your treasure is, there will your heart be also.'

The Challenge of Social Needs

Michael Faraday is also described as being 'most assiduous in visiting the poorer brethren and sisters in their homes, comforting them in their sorrows and afflictions, and assisting them from his own purse. Indeed, he was continually pressed to be the guest of the high and noble, but he would, if possible, decline, preferring to visit some poor sister in trouble, assist her, take a cup of tea with her, read the Bible and pray.'* As will be seen in a later chapter, the social and economic needs of the underprivileged districts in the older parts of Bristol moved A.R.S. to action as much as it had challenged his parents some years before. He was always willing to visit the men of his club at the Shaftesbury in St. Phillip's. The love of God which activated his medical science moved him with similar intensity in helping his neighbour. Part of this strong social interest was certainly due to the example of George Müller.† The last article which he is known to have written reveals the personal veneration in which he held the founder of the Homes at Ashley Down. It is entitled 'George Müller and his Orphanage' and was published in *The Harvester* for September 1953.‡ The opening paragraph reads:

'During the second half of the nineteenth century the life

---

* *Michael Faraday* – James Kendall, 1965 London: Faber & Faber.
† See pages 11f.
‡ See page 33 for an earlier account of the influence of George Müller on Rendle Short's childhood.

and example of George Müller of Bristol were used to strengthen faith all round the world. I have heard my father say that through those years atheism in Bristol scarcely dared to raise its voice, knowing that it would be instantly challenged. It was Müller's mission to show, as he constantly affirmed, that God is still the living God, able and willing to answer prayer. But memories are short; books written over fifty years ago do not get read, especially if they are long. It may be well, therefore, to remind the present generation of the astonishing facts.'

On retirement he had taken time to condense facts from the long original four-volume *Diary of George Müller*, edited by the latter's successor, G. F. Bergin, into a shorter and more readable paperback.¶ The preface reads: 'In my opinion, the example of George Müller's life did more to stimulate active faith in God than did the work or preaching of any other man, during the second half of the nineteenth century. Reasons for this opinion will be given later. So when I was requested to write up the story in a form which might bring it home to the present generation, it seemed a very worth-while task. Excellent books have been written about him, but nothing could be so helpful, so arresting, so calculated to bring tears to the eyes, as George Müller's own diary. The autobiography, besides being out of print, is too large to make easy reading. It seemed best, therefore, to pick out pages and paragraphs here and there, and to supply only a few lines of cementing material, to make the narrative intelligible. It has been a labour of love. I was asked, because my grandfather became a teacher at the Orphanage in 1855; my parents (and countless Bristolians besides) looked up to George Müller all their lives with much the same awe and affection with which the Israelites regarded one of their prophets; and I myself have a few boyish recollections of him, and am well acquainted with his Orphanage.'

Towards the close of this edition of the Diary, A.R.S. writes: 'This record is not intended to glorify George Müller, or even to tell the full story of his life. Its purpose is to illustrate the working out of a principle. The principle is that close obedience to the Will of God, revealed basically in the Bible and day by day in His providential dealings, is rewarded by the fulfilment of His promises. The life of George Müller followed this principle, and was singularly consistent. In his church order, his public service,

¶ *Diary of George Müller,* Edited by A. Rendle Short, 1954, Pickering & Inglis, Glasgow.

his preaching, and his family life, there was just one rule – what does the Bible say?

'We repeat an opinion mentioned in our preface, that in the second half of the nineteenth century he probably exercised an influence in strengthening Christian faith and encouraging Christian living, deeper and more widespread than that of any other man in the world. The scores of thousands of letters, extracts from which were printed in the Reports, prove this. His faith greatly stimulated that of the little group of men who started the Second Evangelical Revival of 1859 in North Ireland, which soon spread all over Britain. Quarrier's Orphan Homes in Scotland, and Barnardo's and Fegan's in England, owed much to his example. There have been similar enterprises in India and Japan. Faith Missions, such as the China Inland Mission, and a dozen or more besides, in other lands, set out to follow the same principles as George Müller had made familiar. The church at Bethesda became a pattern for many more like it all over the world. To this must be added the good done by his sermons, preached to immense congregations, in at least twenty-five countries. The total audience has been estimated at three millions.

'The scientific agnostics of the Victorian era, T. H. Huxley, J. Tyndall and the rest, poured scorn on the idea that praying makes any difference to the course of events, but their theories did not get any great hold in Bristol, under the shadow of the Ashley Down Orphanage. As a donor wrote, it might be interesting if Professor Huxley and his sympathisers who thought prayer a mere waste of breath would try how long they could keep an orphanage going with over 2,000 orphans without asking anyone for help.'

Practical Interest

A.R.S.'s personal interest in the Orphanage has been described by one of the present directors:

'His heart was in it. His interest was deep and personal. The striking personality and almost unique record of the founder's service to God and to the cause of destitute children had deeply impressed him. In spite, therefore, of his many other and diverse interests he became ... a Trustee of the Orphan Homes at Ashley Down. He was always willing to devote much of his time and thought to matters which affected vitally the Homes and to the objects of the Scriptural Knowledge Institution.

'Though so deeply rooted in all the traditions of the work, he was far from being averse to making what seemed to many people drastic changes in it. It was he who first brought the matter definitely before the Trustees and advocated moving from the large barrack-like buildings on Ashley Down to more modern Homes in a country village. He was in full sympathy with the plan to move to a village of Cottage Homes. But when it was suggested that this plan be exchanged for the opening of smaller Homes in various parts of the Bristol area he just as readily agreed to this. Two who have been most closely connected with these changes will never forget how, when a very important decision had quickly to be made regarding a property, the doctor drew them aside to a quiet part in the garden of the house and said, "Let us pray about it." His prayer was characteristically short, intimate, reverent.

'After his retirement, and on hearing that some of our girls and boys were showing an interest in nature study, Mr. Short arranged to take a few of them in his car to the country near Bristol to open to them a little of his great store of knowledge of birds and flowers and geology.'

From as early as 1905 and throughout A.R.S.'s life, whatever moment was not rightfully demanded by his professional work or family, was prodigally given in Christian teaching, preaching and organizing in four main spheres: churches associated with the Brethren, including the work of Müller's Orphan Homes; the Missionary Study Class Movement; services to other Christian communities of Bristol (especially the Shaftesbury Crusade); and the student world. It was perhaps in the Missionary Study Class Movement that he found the deepest springs of action.

The Brethren Movement

By 1908 the time had come when he had to make decisions concerning his church loyalties. He writes – 'Up to this point religious denominations and their different doctrines and practices meant little to me. My views concerning Christian doctrine were of the conservative order, and I did not like anything that savoured of domination by a clerical caste. There were a number of churches, of several complexions, which I could have joined happily. This easy-to-please attitude received a rude jolt when one of these churches had refused to receive me as a medical missionary. The matter evidently had to be looked into. I did look into it, and joined, now of conviction, a congregation, or in their own parlance an "assembly", of the people called "Open Brethren"* I had been received into their communion years before, but that was of convention, with little understanding of the principles involved.

'The general public probably looks upon these people as few in number, freakish in doctrine, austere in manner of life, and often non-cooperative. They are faintly surprised to hear that a scholar like S. P. Tregelles, philanthropists like Dr. Barnardo and George Müller, missionaries like Dan Crawford or Hudson Taylor,† and a distinguished soldier like General Sir William Dobbie, have all been in that communion. Published information about the Brethren is not plentiful and is often inaccurate.

'What is called the "Brethren Movement" is usually described as starting rather over a hundred years ago, in Dublin, followed closely by other circles in Plymouth and Bristol.‡ There has been a continuous succession of such churches from then till now. But there are records, mostly written up by their theological enemies, of isolated bodies of Christians holding very similar principles all down the pages of history from the time of the Apostles. Official Christianity has always disliked them and persecuted them. The Waldenses, the Mennonites, the Ana-baptists and the Stundists¶ have held similar principles, but with various excrescences. The basic idea is quite simple in theory, but difficult to work out in practice. It is that official Christendom has at various points in its history seriously deviated from the apostolic standards. The remedy is to make a determined attempt to form local churches in form and practice as near as possible to those simple communities which are described in the New Testament.

An illustration will serve. If you want a sample of pure drinking water from the river Thames it is useless to take it below Reading or Oxford; you must go as near as possible to the source, i.e. above the point at which the stream has been defiled by the first human habitation. An attentive reading of the New Testament will reveal that each church was at first locally independent and self-governing. There was not a single ordained minister in charge of the congregation, but a group of "elders"; and that there was

---

* See also page 12.
† Founder of the China Inland Mission (now called the Overseas Missionary Fellowship).
‡ See also Appendix II, page 153.
¶ A remarkable movement, which before the Communist Revolution, covered large areas of the farm lands of Southern Russia.

liberty for several to take part in the meeting for worship as they were led by the Spirit, without pre-arrangement. The members were all sharers in the common faith and not mere well-wishers; and they had only two ordinances; baptism, of believers only, and the Lord's Supper, of which all present partook. Great stress was laid upon holiness of life and on vigorous evangelism.

'On these principles the first meetings, separate and un-organized to commence with, were founded, and they have been maintained, with various vicissitudes, ever since. There have been several major differences of opinion and this is one reason why the outsider finds the Brethren difficult to understand. Some meetings are "exclusive", some are "open", some are "intermediate". Some have as little as possible to do with other Christians, others are more co-operative. Halls are often in back streets. Church spires and elaborate frontages are seldom seen. The Brethren usually keep out of politics and big public movements. They dislike being compelled to join trade unions or any such totalitarian com-binations, since that might fetter their freedom of spiritual and ethical action. They do not consider themselves a denomination, they do not themselves use the title of "Plymouth Brethren", and they prefer that of "Christian Brethren".

'It would, therefore, be impossible to say how many groups there are. Probably the largest number, even now, are in Russia. They are thinly scattered over nearly all the countries of Europe, and are plentiful in British Commonwealth countries and in the United States. Distribution over the British Isles is uneven. Assemblies are numerous in the south and west of England and in South Wales, Southern Scotland and Northern Ireland. The force in the foreign missionary field is about a thousand whole-time workers. (*In 1976: c. 1500, of whom c. 600 are from the U.K.*) These are supported by voluntary gifts, but are without any guaranteed salary. In this they endeavour to follow the example of the original Christian preachers. The principal mission fields are Central Africa, Spain, India, Malaya and Central and South America, with the West Indies.

'Membership with such a communion gives abundant op-portunity for lay preaching. There are a few whole-time teachers and evangelists, mostly itinerant, but the main burden of the ministry is sustained by men who earn their own living in some business or profession. This does at least make for keenness, if not always for efficiency.'

Basic Principles

How attached A.R.S. eventually became to the teachings which he had received in earlier years is seen in his having produced in 1913 a book entitled *The Principles of Christians Called 'Open Brethren'* (Pickering & Inglis). It was written under the pseudonym 'A Younger Brother'. The first edition was rapidly exhausted, and a new one called for within three or four months. At the foot of the preface to the second edition the initials 'A.R.S.' have crept in. Already the direct and virile style, which was to become even more vigorous and compelling at a later stage, was making itself felt. It shows itself from the outset of this little volume.

'The principles set forth in this book have been to thousands of saintly souls a mainspring in the busy round of life, and a pillow whereon to rest the weary head of death. They have made missionaries, philanthropists, and (those best of God's ministers on earth) holy, devoted fathers and mothers. They have made men to whom the whole world is under obligation. They are deep-based, rock-ribbed in the fact of Jesus Christ, and the revealed will of God. Now many of these saints have fallen asleep and they hand down to us who follow them their testimony, like the "flaming cross" of Scottish history, bidding us to carry it on to the younger generations rising about us.'

The author also adduces other reasons why the chapters which follow in his book are needed. 'As soon as the little boat leaves the sheltered, land-locked haven of childhood, slips across the bar, and begins to shape its own course out on the wide ocean of life, the hurricane sweeps down upon it – the craving for pleasure, fear of poverty or of isolation, personal sorrow, the difficulty of reconciling modern teaching with old beliefs. But much has been accomplished if one is given grace of the Lord to write or say something that shall help to conserve faith for a few years until it has been made strong by the realization of the presence of the Pilot on board the little craft in some terrifying storm.' He concludes his Preface by apologizing – characteristically – for any harsh word which might seem to judge others – 'It takes very uncommon grace to write convincingly where one feels strongly, without seeming to lack in charity towards those who differ.'

In this early volume are harbingers of things to come. Robust common sense, an incisive mind and wide reading, com-

bine to produce a straightforward and uncompromising defence of
the simple Christianity of the community in which he was cradled.
A.R.S. never despised true learning or research in any of its forms.
But he kept it in its place as the handmaid and not the master of the
Christian minister. He had already had ample evidence in his own
experience of what St. Paul meant in his classic description of the
source of true wisdom* He now gives an early foretaste of his
realism and power vividly to bring home to his hearers the crucial
principles involved.

   'When Paul heard what painful meetings the Christians
were having in Corinth he might have said "Do not listen any
longer to all these ignorant people, mostly slaves. Make Stephanas
your minister and let him do it all." No doubt this would have
helped very much in some directions, but the apostle was not
prepared to give up the open meeting. It was far too valuable. He
did not want to make churches like comets, with a brilliant head
and a long nebulous tail. He told them, however – and it is very important to put the injunction into practice – that the assembly was
not called upon to listen to everybody who chose to make himself a
nuisance, or who talked unprofitably. There were some "whose
mouths must be stopped" (Tit. 1:11). The listeners were to be the
judges (I Cor. 14:27–29). It was an open meeting, but there were
rules to be obeyed. It was a meeting open for the Spirit to speak by
whom He would, not open for men to say what they pleased.

   'It may be asked, "But is it not better to sit under the
ministry of university graduates who have been trained to preach
than to have to listen to business men, or even uneducated persons?" Paul said, "Knowledge puffeth up, but love buildeth up."
God hath chosen the *poor* of this world, rich in faith. "Not many
wise, not many noble, are called." He hath hidden things from the
wise and prudent that are revealed unto babes. Whilst not un-
der-estimating the value of good education, wide culture and experience in ministry, and the importance of giving time to prepare
for preaching, yet these are quite secondary matters. Grace is not
necessarily learned in colleges. I amuse myself sometimes by looking over the examination papers for university degrees in theology.
I should rather think that to answer some of the questions on
critical subjects would involve a shipwreck, either of faith in God's
Word, or of the examination result!'

* I Cor 1:18–2:16.

As Christian Leader

Though A.R.S.'s lay preaching had a considerable appeal for middle-aged and elderly people, especially to the plain men in St. Phillip's, Bristol, yet his chief impact was upon the younger generation. This remained so right up to the end of his life. This essentially shy man, who lived all his life in his own city in the West Country, was destined to sow the seeds of Christian teaching in the hearts and minds of many in other parts of the world. Many younger lives coming into contact with him became thoroughly armed spiritually and morally for what awaited them in the wider world.

His connection with the Stokes Croft assembly is of more than passing interest. According to a former member, 'In those days a very large congregation attended. Mr. E. R. Short (A.R.S.'s father) was prominent from the start, and although he had worked at Wagg's mission for twenty-eight years, he later became the superintendent of the Sunday School for twelve years and carried on his connection with the adult work up until near the time of his death at the age of ninety-six. It was therefore appropriate that on the Jubilee of Stokes Croft Chapel in July 1929 A.R.S. should be the speaker, his father having spoken to the Sunday School in the afternoon. It is also of interest that it was A.R.S. who on Sunday, November 24th in 1941 had just opened the last of a series of special addresses when the sirens heralded the first heavy bombing attack on Bristol. Stokes Croft Chapel was that night severely damaged by blast and in a subsequent raid destroyed.'

When for professional reasons he had moved to reside in Clifton, he became a leader at the old Bethesda Chapel, Great George Street, at the foot of Brandon Hill. In 1915 he also became a member of the united 'oversight', which was responsible for the care of four assemblies, viz. Bethesda, Alma Road, Stokes Croft and Totterdown. Following that disastrous Sunday evening in November when Bethesda Chapel was also destroyed by enemy bombing, the Alma Road assembly in Clifton became from then, until his death, his spiritual home and the centre of his preaching ministry.

The First & Second Address

A.R.S. first led a meeting at Sevier Street in 1894, i.e. when he was fourteen years old. His notes for the second occasion were found on a small discoloured piece of notepaper in fading ink. A later note has been added at the foot which states – 'This was my first *prepared* paper or address (the first of all was impromptu, in 1894, at Sevier Street). Date probably 1894. Given at the Y.M.C.A. Youth Club, Bristol.'

'Works, and Their Relationship to Salvation'. R. Short
(Read Jas. 2:14 to end)

'Works, like faith, must be real or false, in other words, living or dead; and works, to be living, must be backed up by living faith, as faith, to be living, must be backed up by living works. Jas. 2:26, and many other verses in the same chapter which we have just read. It is by faith we can be saved. (Rom. 3:28; 5:1; Gal. 2:16; 3:24) But since there can be no real faith without works, without works it is impossible to be justified, and though we cannot enter heaven *because* of our good works (Eph. 2:9), yet they are a sign of faith, as we are frequently told in Jas. 2, and thus indirectly save.

'Bernard, a great divine of the early Church, many of whose writings have come down to us, said "Good works are the way to the kingdom, not the cause of reigning in it". There are many ways of doing good to those around. Perhaps you can visit a sick man and read to him a bit; at any rate you can do your duties to the best of your ability, to the glory of God.

' "Content to fill a little space
If Thou be glorified."

'Besides glorifying your Master and giving unmistakable evidence of your faith, these little (if little they can be called) services will exercise a great influence for good over yourself, making you stronger in the Christian life and ready to do more. But if you would be a successful worker you must prefer to be a listener to God's instruction in private, or you will go wrong. Even Christ, the pattern Christian worker, never lost an opportunity to slip away from the boisterous crowd and the noisy city to be alone with His Father in prayer on the silent hilltop. He did not do this when He was needed by the people, however, but did not object to rising early in the morning, before anybody else was up.

'The Bible is full of commands to work (Col. 1:10; Heb. 10:24, 13:21; 2 Thes. 2:17; Phil. 2:12, and many others), but the punishment for works without faith is awful (Gal. 3:10; Jer 48:7). But every blessing will attend living works, therefore let us toil on, unwearied by the strife. How many of us will be able to say with St. Paul, as we stand on the brink of death (surrounded by discouragements and trials, as he was, with nearly all his old friends leaving him and going after false teachers): "I have fought a good fight, I have finished my course, I have kept the faith; henceforth there is laid up for me a crown of righteousness, which the Lord, the righteous judge, shall give me at that day"? Remember our every action has some influence on others. God helps us to walk worthily. Remember Jas. 1:25. Finally, "Commit thy works unto the Lord, and thy thoughts shall be established" (Pr. 16:3).'

The Later Style

Examples of his later developed style are to be found in *Why Believe?* (1938 edition). If the last four paragraphs of this book be read aloud with deliberation and emphasis, the reader can receive a fair impression of the way in which he would later close one of his Sunday evening sermons. These would often end abruptly, much as this book does:—

'No doubt someone will say that we are making the Way too complicated. Many persons have undoubtedly become Christians who had no idea at the time that they were following the directions of these five groups of passages. But we must not complain if a life-saving prescription contains four or five different but necessary medicines. It would be folly to leave some out. And on consideration the Way is not complicated. It amounts to this: the acceptance, by an act of faith, of Jesus Christ as our personal Saviour, bringing in forgiveness and cleansing from our sins by His atoning death; and also as our God and Master. He is therefore to be worshipped and reverenced as God, and followed and obeyed as Lord. That is to say, he is to be accepted in full character, for all that he claimed to be.

'But will mere "believing" in this sense have such a far--reaching effect? Yes. It is like the act of pressing an electric switch and of liberating power. It acts on the man himself. Realizing that his sin sent Jesus to the Cross, and having now taken Him as Master, he hates his old sinful path and follows Christ's way of life. This changes his plans, his friendships, his amusements, his business dealings, his behaviour at home, everything. It is repentance, conversion.

'But our resolution is weak; shall we not soon fail? No; faith, so to speak, presses another switch. Jesus Christ, as an invited and permanent Guest, enters the life to empower, to purify, to impart joy and peace and love. As a crab-apple tree may be made to bear luscious fruit by ingrafting from a good stock, so He is willing to come into our lives, and to bring in His own qualities.

'The great thing is to make a definite decision. How? Well, here is a method that has helped thousands. Take pen and paper. Write down what is to be the relation of the Lord Jesus Christ to you. Make two copies. Post one to some one else, relative, friend, pastor or some quite unexpected person. *And keep the other yourself.'*

Wider Influence

Throughout his life A.R.S. preached on almost every Sunday evening and sometimes also in the afternoons. Occasionally he would be absent from Bristol at a conference or special meeting. He almost never preached away from Bristol on the Sunday mornings, reserving this time for worship together with the family. Frequently, however, particularly between the wars, he would give a short homily at the close of the normal period of worship at the old Bethesda Chapel on Brandon Hill. Some of them – expanded a little – would have adorned a university pulpit.

From time to time he would preach in almost all the Brethren places of worship in the Bristol area. He was also frequently a guest preacher in the country areas around in Gloucester and Somerset. His visits were well remembered by the elders of any given place, not least because of the one feature in the organization required. It was understood by anyone engaging his services that there must always be a member of the local church prepared to start the service and to carry on until he arrived. Though he was frequently detained by emergencies until the service's commencement, he always contrived to arrive in time to give the sermon. Occasionally he would come straight up into the pulpit after the commencement of the service, having travelled by car a good many miles. His habit, then, was quietly to sit down and bow his head for some two minutes. Then he would reveal his gift for detaching himself completely from all that had earlier been occupying his mind, and would give of his best to the waiting congregation.

One local elder has recorded his feelings on one occasion when it had fallen to him to start the service. Hymns, prayer and readings of Scripture had all been completed. The hymn before the sermon had been announced and it was already being sung. A.R.S. had not arrived! In a turmoil of mind he was in the midst of preparing a hasty apology and a short extempore 'sermon'. The final verse of the hymn had actually started when, to his immense relief, the door opened and a seemingly unconcerned figure walked quietly up the aisle and enabled him to make a hasty retreat from the pulpit!

Nor was it simply a matter of going to preach. He made himself very much a part of the community. A missionary on furlough has written:

'My memories of Dr. Rendle Short are centred mainly in the happy church fellowship of Bethesda Chapel, Great George Street. I was impressed by his unfailing regularity at the meeting for worship on Sunday morning when he took his place in the family pew. He graciously followed on any faltering efforts of younger men with a simple but effectual leading to the point of our worship, and then at the Table in a dignified and fatherly manner he broke the bread. He often did so. Indeed, the great love and respect for him as a true "bishop" among us led us to expect him to minister in this way.

'His contributions to the weekly Bible readings were often very original, but always scriptural. One that comes to my mind was entitled "Joseph's bones"* from which he discussed the faithfulness of God in fulfilling His promises. He was nearly always at the Monday evening prayer meetings, if he was in the city, however busy his day may have been at the B.R.I. His sincere, factual prayers followed a survey of the subjects for prayer. He encouraged us to have an interest in the many activities in which he and others were engaged. The fact that he continued this meeting for prayer in his own home for twelve years or more after Bethesda Chapel had been destroyed by fire during the war was an indication of its value to him. The faithfulness of his personal prayer was disclosed when we learned of his daily remembrance of several missionaries, which included ourselves.'

Interest in Younger Age Groups

Many accounts of his various forms of influence were written at the time of his death, one or two extracts from which

* Genesis 50: 25, 26.

may be given: 'His realization of the importance of youth was constantly being shown. There was, for example, his interest in the efforts which the young people at Bethesda made to run a children's service in a small hall in a depressed neighbourhood. He helped with the rent and the gas bill. Sometimes, also, he would go out to Brandon Hill on summer Sunday evenings to join for a while in the open-air meetings.'

'It was quite usual to see him arriving at the Chapel on his cycle which he said "prevented him from getting stout". Coming by cycle also allowed him the pleasure of walking, often with some of us younger ones, through the gardens laid out below the Cabot Tower. It was no little surprise to find that he knew the names of all the plants as well as he knew the back of his own hand. He would inspect the flowers with us right up to the Tower and then with a short "good-bye" climbed down the hill to his cycle and was off to his home, or down to the B.R.I. again.

'Those who knew him best could give numerous examples of his deep and carefully nourished love for young children. He would address Sunday Schools on such objects as black lead pencils, or magnets. Or, he might illustrate his talk with quite elaborate chemical experiments. Nothing was too much trouble to arrest the imagination and then to instruct the young mind. He had a way of captivating the interest of children of all ages.' A Sunday School superintendent writes: 'We stood on the door-step one Sunday afternoon to welcome him, with a message from the leader of the primary School, whose two or three dozen scholars were all under eight. The question I had to ask was, would he be able to manage the younger as well as the older scholars? If not, they would go to their own room. He nodded his assent, that it would be quite all right for them to stay. The afternoon was a complete success.'

Impact on Youth

The following example of his speaking style is taken from an address given to three thousand young people in London:*

'How foolish you would think a quarryman who was content with getting out stones in a quarry by explosion and by pick and chisel, if he were to leave the stones lying loose in the quarry. The stones were taken out that they might be formed into a building. They were brought out in vain unless they fulfil their pur-

* In Spurgeon's Tabernacle, Newington Butts, London in November 1924: ('The Witness', January 1925).

pose, and it is the purpose of the Lord that those who are "born again" should be brought together into the Christian fellowship. When we come to compare New Testament principles with modern practice we find a sad contrast. There are churches today where few or no questions would be asked as to whether those who apply to join them have been "born again" or not. Of course, with the utmost care in the world mistakes may be made. Church examiners are not infallible. They may sometimes *include* someone whom the Lord has not included and they may sometimes *exclude* someone whom He has included. But there ought to be a godly attempt to sort out the wheat from the chaff in this connection.

'Now the principles of fellowship in the New Testament churches were neither too lax nor too exclusive. Errors have been made in both directions. There are an enormous number of passages in the New Testament exhorting us to love and unity with all true believers. You may turn over chapter after chapter, page after page, and find exhortations to that effect ... Yet we know that sometimes Christians have excluded one another on totally inadequate grounds, grounds as flimsy as those we read of in the third Epistle of John, where Diotrephes turned some out of the Church on purely personal grounds, and it became a matter of individual opinion, and sometimes of individual spite, instead of Scriptural principles. Let us seek carefully that we receive even those weak in the faith, and not sit in judgment upon their doubts. Let us, therefore, receive all whom Christ has received, except those whom He has expressly put under discipline.'

In his own personal practice A.R.S. set young people a fine example. He had, what many lack, a sense of proportion and due balance in his approach to the Christian faith, speaking and organizing. He avoided enthusiasm of the wrong kind, but did not fail in being fervent in his own spirit. He could be relied upon to give a balanced and accurate statement about any subject, and he was always a restraining influence on irresponsible and extreme views. On one occasion an over-pious young man had given it as his opinion that every Christian should make it a rule to rise at 6 o'clock each morning to read the Bible and pray. When he had finished A.R.S. quietly commented: 'Remember that what is not laid down as a *command* in the Bible is never right for everybody.'

Unobtrusive Charity

His financial services to missionaries came to light only

after his death when the volume of letters of grateful memories had begun to grow. Then it became obvious how faithful a steward of his money he had been. Missionaries on furlough, of course, had been surgically treated without fee; but (what was not so obvious) nursing home fees, too, had a way of being absurdly small when they tried to make their payment. It was also his habit to operate without fee on members of the Christian ministry. The vicar of a poor parish, who had enquired why no account of fees had been sent, was told: 'When you are made a bishop you shall pay me: meanwhile I should like to take the payment in your prayers for me.' Another Christian minister, who had inherited a little money and liked to be financially independent, tried to persuade him to take a fee. At last a gift to a religious charity, which both admired, proved an acceptable compromise.

He was chairman of several trusts for the maintenance of buildings for Christian worship. He himself had pioneered several of them and given considerable sums for building chapels in the areas around Bristol. The building of a new chapel at Sea Mills on a new housing estate was entirely the result of his single-mindedness. He was out for a cycle ride one Saturday afternoon when he discovered that the town planning authority had made no reservations for church buildings on the estate. He at once set to work and took the initiative in purchasing a plot for a "Brethren" hall and also notified the leaders of the different denominations of the fact that they would not be represented in this estate if they did not hasten to claim a site.

At the time of his death, the leader of a congregation in Somerset, asked whether A.R.S. had contributed anything to their building replied in a broad Somerset accent: 'Stands to reason he paid for it. You can't have a hall if you haven't got the ground.' On hearing of vacant ground in this area, he had immediately sent a cheque in order to secure it.

Further evidence of much unobtrusive generosity was gleaned from one of his intimate friends with whom he regularly discussed the relative needs of the religious and charitable objects which he supported.

'He frequently used me as a go-between. Invariably, when I would speak to him about some contemplated project he would say, "We will call a meeting, you make the suggestions, I will gladly support you". He was always the first to send a handsome subscription and would ask me to let him know if there was any deficit when the work was finished. Unknown to others he frequently footed the final bill.

'I well remember one incident. He visited a village about ten miles from Bristol for the purpose of speaking at a meeting in a house. It had been held there for a number of years. He happened to learn that the tenant of the house was about to vacate it because he could no longer maintain the rent and had been unable to raise a loan to buy it at the price asked. The next morning Mr. Short telephoned to ask me to go to the village to see what could be done. I had authority to buy the house at the price asked and to tell the tenants that they could still remain at a nominal rent to be paid to me. I made it clear it was a Christian man who would be their landlord, but that all their dealings were to be with me.

'This was not the end of the story. The tenant had been almost ruined during the depression but with the return of better times his business began to improve and he saved enough money to be able to buy the house. The property had doubled or trebled its value because of post-war conditions. About this time Mr. Short preached at a service held in the house and found that the tenant was now better placed. Again he instructed me to go down later in the week to tell the tenant that if he wished to purchase the house he could. When I suggested to him that the value of property was now at least double or treble he said "Tell them that they can have it at the same price as I paid for it". I have reason to know that they never guessed who the benefactor actually was. Not long before his death he gave a large sum of money to build a chapel in an overseas country where the Christians had lost their meeting places because of persecution.'

Local Speaking and Preaching

In 1947 it was suggested that a 'Bible School' should be started in Bristol and on hearing of the proposition, A.R.S. was at once enthusiastic. He immediately suggested an outline of a scheme for study, and was full of ideas about the speakers, the methods of work and note-taking. He would happily come along to speak at very short notice if one of the lecturers failed to turn up. Year by year he worked assiduously in connection with this school. It was extremely profitable to hear his own lectures, especially those on Genesis and Isaiah.

These were based on a rigorous study of the Bible. Dr. F. F.

Bruce, Rylands Professor of Biblical Criticism in the University of Manchester, writes:

'Professor Rendle Short would never have claimed to be a Biblical specialist. But a man with his upbringing, intellectual gifts, and sterling Christian faith could not but be a Bible student, and Bible study was one of the serious pursuits of his life. The better to equip himself for Bible study, he acquired a competent familiarity with the original languages, and while his knowledge of Greek and Hebrew was something which he would never have dreamed of parading, it would have put many professional "Ministers of the Word" to shame.

'In conversation and correspondence he revealed from time to time how carefully he had considered some of the outstanding problems of Biblical introduction and interpretation. At one time I had some discussion by letter with him on the subject of Gospel criticism. He showed clearly how attentively he had examined this subject, and his conclusions (whether they would command general assent among Biblical critics or not) were conclusions which he had reached after a judicial weighing of the evidence.

'His understanding of the Biblical message made him a greatly appreciated Bible teacher on many a public platform, and his lucid and logical style made many a difficult problem seem easy when he expounded it. There are, to be sure, some hearers who like Bible addresses to be somewhat above their heads, couched in involved language which they don't quite grasp. Such hearers were sometimes misled by Rendle Short's orderly presentation and use of the simplest English words into thinking it strange that a man of such repute should not deal with "deep" subjects when teaching the Bible! But there was a quality about his public ministry which made it stick in the mind. I have very clear recollections of addresses which I heard him give between twenty and twenty-five years ago, including two powerful gospel addresses, delivered one after the other in Aberdeen on the first Sunday evening of 1932, on the texts "supposing him to have been in the company" (Lk 2:44) and "beginning to sink" (Mt. 14:30). In all his speaking it was plain that he was giving the fruit of his own independent study; no one could describe Rendle Short as an adherent of any particular school. And it was characterized throughout by the spiritual power of a man of God, who had the spiritual welfare of his hearers greatly at heart. Nowhere was this more evident than at young people's conferences; there are many Christians who have had epoch-making dealings with God because of Rendle Short's talks on such occasions.

'His Biblical knowledge was made available to wider circles by his writings. In one of the earliest (perhaps the earliest) purely religious books he wrote – *The Principles of Christians Called "Open Brethren"* – he devoted the opening chapters not to questions of ecclesiastical doctrine and polity, but to an exposition of the basic Christian truths, such as the deity of Christ, the authority of the Bible, and the essence of the gospel, These were subjects which he continued to expound throughout his life, especially with a view to removing difficulties which beset young people who think seriously about them. What he could have achieved had he devoted himself to Biblical exegesis may be guessed from his little book *In the Days of the Prophet Isaiah,* in which he shows rare skill in reconstructing the life and general atmosphere of Jerusalem towards the end of the eighth century B.C., as the background to Isaiah's ministry.

'But in his written as in his spoken ministry Rendle Short had one prime object. "We must decide in some way about Jesus Christ", runs a chapter-title in one of his books; and as he himself had early decided about Him in the right way, his dominant passion was so to present Him to others that they, too, might reach the decision to enthrone Him in their hearts as Saviour and sovereign Lord.'

At the time of the 1951 Jubilee Exhibition in Bristol he was invited to trace the history of the Brethren in the city, during the past hundred years. Those who heard it will never forget the compelling way in which he told the story. He had brought with him George Müller's Bible and also had numerous pictures of other outstanding figures who have lived and worked in the city. Finally, a picture was shown of George Müller's funeral in 1898, with the immense crowds who lined the streets as a tribute to his fame and work.

A.R.S. was often at his best on a Sunday evening when he went out into the country districts of Gloucester or Somerset to some small chapel, where would be gathered a congregation of anything up to twenty-five or thirty of the local folk. Many of them he could address by name. He was quite free and at home, indulging in the crystal clear illustrations which he loved to use on such occasions. Pulling his well-worn pocket Bible from the tail of his frock coat, he would now discourse in plain Anglo-Saxon. It did not matter how far the distance, how bad the weather, how small the congregation, how feeble the work, or how poor the state of the building. It was remarkable that such a popular speaker, who could draw a crowd in almost any church, chapel or hall in Bristol, could be equally happy in these small communities. It was on this account that he became so beloved in the surrounding West Country.

On these occasions there would be no discussions of the difficulties of biblical interpretation. Gone were his Hebrew and Greek. He was as intent as Tyndale — who always had been one of his heroes — in his anxiety to ensure that the knowledge of the Scriptures should extend 'to him that driveth the plough'. Taking as his subject a simple parable, or miracle or discourse of Christ, he would draw vivid lessons which his hearers never forgot.

The leader of one such country community recalls that early on one February Sunday evening, when snow was thick on the ground, he had telephoned to Bristol. He pointed out that it was a bad night, it was a long way to come, and that probably only six or seven people might be at the service. A.R.S. simply replied 'When does the service start?' On being told, he firmly said 'I'll be there'.

CHAPTER 11

Defender of the Faith

*'Belief in God gives us greater elasticity of
mind.'*
H. *Butterfield*

*'An account of the world, in this one single view,
as God's world.'*
J. *Butler*

'I have often speculated', said A.R.S. at the close of a student conference in 1932* 'concerning the choice the apostle Paul
would have made if he were alive today, in determining his sphere
of service for the Lord Jesus Christ. I have a strong suspicion that
he would make straight for some of our large universities. Which of
them he would choose, I cannot say; but I suspect that they are
where he would go. It is very noteworthy in the New Testament
records how he selected the strategic centres. There was only one
of these (Alexandria) which, so far as we know, he did not succeed
in reaching. He sought those points where gathered men and
women, whose influences were likely to be far-reaching. Such
points are found in the universities today. At these are being
trained the leaders of the future – the school teachers and the
college professors; the doctors, the preachers, the writers, the
administrators, and a large number of athletes (who often get a
hearing where scholars fail to do so, especially amongst young
people).'

This conviction caused him year after year regularly to send
a letter over his signature to several Christian periodicals, asking
"freshmen" to send in their names to the respective university
Christian Unions or to the secretary of the Inter-Varsity
Fellowship. One such letter, signed by him, appeared fourteen days

---

* He was one of the Senior Members who had encouraged the formation of student
Christian Unions, and the Inter-Varsity Fellowship uniting them, in the post-war years
1919–1927.

after his death and must have been among the last of the letters he wrote. It was entitled 'To Christian Freshmen':

'You have come up to the university. Some of you can say "again". To others it is all very fresh and exciting; quite an adventure. You are a member of some Christian Church, and you realize that it is your duty to engage in Christian service. You believe in the great historic doctrines of the faith, and accept the authority of the Bible. Now, the question arises, in what direction are you going to make your real offensive? Which is to be the "containing attack" and which the main objective? Work for Christ inside, or outside, the university?

'No doubt, the latter will be the path of least resistance. It is a beaten track. It is easy to talk to your social and intellectual inferiors. They are not so likely to answer back, for one thing. But just consider for a minute.

'Generally speaking, students can be reached only by students and by those for whom they themselves create an opportunity. If you don't do it, it will not be done. You have only three or four years in which to attempt the problem; you may have thirty or forty years for those other people. Students are peculiarly open to impressions. A university course leaves a deep mark on most men and women. Probably it will on you. Most students are completely changed during their undergraduate days; and, thank God, we have often seen them changed for Him, or, to use an old-fashioned (but expressive) word, "converted" '.

Support for the Christian Unions

In an article concerning the Evangelical Movement in Universities entitled 'The Place of the I.V.F. in the World of Tomorrow', A.R.S. allowed his enthusiasm free rein. It was written in 1944, when the war was just beginning to turn clearly in favour of the Western allies and possibilities of reconstruction were beginning to be discussed:

'The Christian Unions had very humble beginnings. I well remember at the end of the 1914–18 war, seeing very plainly the need for a conservative, evangelical witness in the universities and wondering how anything could possibly be done to begin it. The C.I.C.C.U.* was, of course, in existence, but there was little or nothing elsewhere, as far as I knew. Then, one by one, little groups

* The Cambridge Intercollegiate Christian Union.

arose. The stories of some of these origins have been told in print. I personally was in at the beginning of some of them — Bristol, Exeter, Glasgow, Birmingham. There was plenty of cold water, but once started, nearly all the Unions were maintained. In one or two cities they allowed themselves to be submerged by uniting with other causes which had no definite doctrinal basis and were without a soul-saving message. But by and by a new start was made on right lines. How small the original united Conferences were! How scanty our finances — less than a hundred pounds a year had to cover all central expenses. If it had not been for the faithful service of our early officers, humanly speaking, all co-ordination would have been given up long ago, and more Unions would have disappeared or failed to develop. It is very difficult for people who have only known the Unions and the Fellowship as they are today to realize how small things were only twenty years ago. But the movement was of God, and it was bound to go on.'

Amongst the latest additions to A.R.S.'s autobiographical papers are many notes which show his abiding sense of the importance of the work which he did among students:—

'It has been one of my greatest pleasures and privileges to visit groups for Christian witness and fellowship in universities and colleges and medical schools in all parts of the British Isles. Students, however, are not always very business-like in their arrangements for speakers (though they have improved vastly of late)! They have their whims and fancies. One of my experiences must be very unusual. I had been invited to address one group of students in the East of England, and another in Wales, at about the same time. But on the self-same day I received letters from both of the secretaries cancelling my engagements, one because they had been informed that I "believed in the verbal inspiration of the Bible", and the other because their information was that I did not. I had some thoughts of exchanging the letters and posting them back to their opposite destinations, but this seemed likely to lead to interminable correspondence for which I had no time. So I decided to turn the other cheek and bear the double affront meekly. But students come and students go, and I have visited both places many times since with no further accusation levelled.'

First Student Activities in Bristol

A.R.S.'s début as an organizer of student meetings and as speaker to students began early in his post-graduate years. He had

had some contact with the Student Volunteer Movement for Foreign Missions and he had organized several public missionary meetings for students. But after his marriage and when still Registrar at the Royal Infirmary, he commenced special meetings for Bristol students. The first and most enduring of these was a meeting for prayer. It was run by students in his own home, and later moved with him to 69 Pembroke Road. This meeting took place every Sunday of term at 10 a.m. It commenced in 1909 and continued up to the time of his death. He seldom went in to these meetings himself, in order to leave the students free to conduct them in their own way.

During the years 1911 to 1914, he organized a very popular series of addresses at the Victoria Rooms. The speaker on the first occasion was Dan Crawford, a pioneer missionary in Central Africa and author of *Thinking Black*. Those meetings were announced in well-printed leaflets and were in the nature of after-church services on the Sunday evenings. With the invitation to the meeting went one to a buffet supper so that the students who attended the city churches could come on directly to the hall. The series usually occupied four consecutive Sundays in the Michaelmas Term and four in the Lent Term. Sometimes there were as many as 200 to 250 students present. In these A.R.S. had not only the help of Mrs. Rendle Short and a team of women helpers handling the catering, but of Dr. Frank Bergin, radiologist at the Bristol General Hospital, and of W. R. Moore, a retired barrister who was at that time resident in Bristol. Mr. Moore later moved to Oxford where his 'Open House' became justly famous among Christian undergraduates between the years 1924 and 1936.

From time to time letters were received from many grateful former Bristol students. One was received during the 1914–18 war having come via Spain, and addressed to Mrs. Short by a German student from a well-known family. He had been entertained at these meetings in the pre-war years. The expressions of sincere appreciation fell down somewhat owing to the peculiarities of the English language. It was appreciated all the more fully. It ended 'When this darkness has past, I will return to your ghastly home and be fed up with your much food.'(!)

After the outbreak of war in 1914 the series of special addresses was temporarily discontinued. When re-started in 1919, they lasted but a few months, because in 1921 the Bristol

Inter-Faculty Christian Union came into being and from then on began to arrange its own meetings in the Victoria Rooms. A.R.S. was, however, invited to be the first President of the B.I.F.C.U. and was repeatedly invited to speak to its open meetings. He rarely failed to draw a large crowd. From time to time he also spoke at the 'squashes' for students and young people which were held in the houses of Dr. Frank Bergin and Colonel Middleton West. He was also one of the most popular of the speakers at week-end conferences held by the Christian Union in Dr. Bergin's large bungalow and surrounding buildings, situated on the Somerset coast at Walton near Clevedon. In the years leading up to 1939, 'Bergo's Bung', as the students called it, became quite an institution. The free time during the afternoons became alive to new interests when A.R.S. began to share his overflowing knowledge of birds and natural history. He lost no time in directing heedless eyes to the more striking phenomena of biology, geology and other branches of natural science. One of the first members of the Bristol Christian Union commented as he looked back on his student days:–

'Few of us who were in B.I.F.C.U. in its early years will forget the help Professor Rendle Short gave us in those days of struggling. He was president of the Union; he let his drawing-room be used on Sunday afternoons for the Bible Studies, a good proportion of these he was invited to address. He was always ready to meet us and give his helpful advice on matters of policy and practice. Financially he more than once assisted our meagre funds to meet the liabilities. He proved to be one upon whom you could always fall back, always patient, and never at a loss for an answer to the students' questions.'

Influence in other Universities

His interests extended to most of the other universities. Christian students from Oxford, Cambridge, and the London Medical Schools, with several of the civic universities, had established in 1919 what became known as the 'Inter-Varsity Conference'. A.R.S. quickly saw the importance of the conference, and he early became a regular and trusted speaker. In his later years he maintained a close association with it. He was one of the first Senior Members on the committees of the 1920–22 period. He was also asked to join the first Advisory Committee, of which he retained his membership until the time of his death. In 1928, when

an organization known as the Inter-Varsity Fellowship* developed
as a permanent extension of the conference, he was one of the first
elected Vice-Presidents and also became the Senior Treasurer. He
was later twice made President and gave two valuable presidential
addresses at the annual conference. His tenure of the post of Senior
Treasurer was more than nominal for he had provided the first (and
for several years the only) regular income of the movement. Early
conference organizers have vivid memories of the 'Rendelian' £20
cheque which annually arrived to pay for speakers' expenses and to
help some of the more impecunious students to attend by affording
them part-hospitality. Twenty pounds in those days went a long
way!

In the interests of these student Christian Unions A.R.S.
travelled at one time or another to almost every university in the
British Isles. He would go as far as Aberdeen. Indeed he was so
acceptable as a speaker that the Unions in Birmingham, London
and Aberdeen elected him as one of their own Vice-Presidents and
repeatedly invited him to speak for them. On two occasions he
completed a 'tour' of the Scottish universities.

Students in the twelve London Medical Schools had their
own special reasons for being grateful for his help. He would
seldom fail to make a speaking engagement for one of them each
time that some academic or other important reason was bringing
him to London. At one time the London students so relied on him
that he was familiarly known in their circles as 'our Hon. Senior
Travelling Secretary'! In his talks he would always take up for
them questions which were not at the time being tackled by other
speakers – as for instance special problems concerning the authority of the Bible, evolution and psychology. He was similarly of
special help to the colleges of education, where the students found
his clear answers to their questions of special value. He would,
therefore, disregard any inconvenience to be a regular visitor at
their students' house party at Ambleside each July.

Several of the university Christian Unions owe their origin
to his timely initiatives. The first president of one has written:

'Well do I remember† how Professor Rendle Short was one
of the decisive (though behind-the-scenes) links in the founding of

---

* Now the Universities and Colleges Christian Fellowship.

† It is interesting to notice that, in their letters, the correspondents who were most
influenced by him commence 'I well remember' and go on to use a number of A.R.S.'s
characteristic phrases.

the Birmingham University Evangelical Christian Union. Three Birmingham students were at the annual Inter-Varsity Conference at High Leigh, Hoddesdon, Herts. He could only attend for a little over one day, and during those hours had to speak several times. However, he made time to call the three of us together, and, sitting on a bench in the garden, he suggested how we could set about the formation of a Christian Union in Birmingham. I can see him now, framing the words which afterwards went up on the university notice board, asking those "who hold the more conservative views of the Christian faith" to meet to discuss the situation. Those words, and that notice, bore fruit, and the Christian Union came into existence the following term.'

Many of A.R.S.'s aphorisms and stories lived on in the student minds of his audiences. His words had a habit of sticking: 'The nearer you are to a light the darker is your shadow. Thus the one who has the greatest light is often the most conscious of wrong in himself.' 'The purpose of prayer is not to be a kind of penny-in-the-slot machine, but to conform our wills to the will of God.' Of Archippus, a comparatively unknown figure in the Bible, he would say 'He was not first violin, but second fiddle, always a most difficult instrument to play.'

Defending the Faith

Whilst not a few men and women were turned by him from a life of self-indulgence to a life of righteousness, A.R.S.'s chief function in the student world was as a defender of the Christian faith. On his contribution in this field, F. F. Bruce comments:

'He had no time for the "unfounded notion that our faith must be believed in the teeth of proved facts to the contrary", and no sympathy with the *credo quia absurdum* attitude of some contemporary theologians. Apologetics he believed to be a valuable and necessary Christian discipline, and it was one for which he was unusually gifted. "Faith will be unstable," he maintained, "and for many persons impossible, if we cannot say that 'we have not followed cunningly devised fables'."

'In a series of books – *The Historic Faith in the Light of Today* (written in collaboration with B. Colgrave), *The Bible and Modern Research, Modern Discovery and the Bible, Why Believe?* and *Archaeology Gives Evidence* – he set himself to assure undergraduates and other thinking young people that there was nothing in modern knowledge which stood in the way of a sincere and intelligent Christian faith. He dealt not only with the Christian view of the natural sciences, but showed a sound grasp of current trends in Biblical history and criticism. When *The Bible and Modern Research* appeared, the Principal of a well-known theological college in Scotland, an eminent theologian himself, recommended it to his students as a textbook in apologetics.

'Rendle Short was not the only scientist to write on science and the Bible. Too many scientists who have done this, however, have failed because their understanding of the Bible, unlike their scientific attainments, had hardly advanced beyond the Sunday School stage. This is perhaps particularly evident in many attempts to relate the creation narratives of Genesis to geological and anthropological knowledge. But one did not feel this about Rendle Short's work; he had examined the Biblical text in a spirit of scholarly inquiry, and even if Biblical specialists saw reason to dissent from his arguments, they recognized that they must be treated with respect.

'On the relations between his own professional interest and Christian belief he contributed two authoritative and fascinating books to the "Second Thoughts Library" of the Paternoster Press – *Wonderfully Made* and *The Bible and Modern Medicine*. He was a man of many parts, and would have adorned any profession he chose to enter.'

Many students between the two world wars, whose feet had begun to slip because of an unresolved intellectual conflict, were restored to *terra firma* by the robust common sense and infectious faith of A.R.S. He possessed an unusual forcefulness compounded of a direct didactic approach, which bespoke intellectual honesty in religious matters, combined with a practical understanding and a warm heart which beat true to all the basic things of Christian belief. An example of his method of dealing with such subjects as the creation and the origin of man when talking to students is to be found on pages 88–118 of his book *Modern Discovery and the Bible*. The following is taken from pp. 100–102:

'That the main purpose of the narrative of the creation in Genesis is to show God as the Creator, that the terms used are popular and even symbolical and not those of exact science (how could they be, in such an ancient writing?), we heartily agree; but that the information conveyed is incorrect we as heartily deny. Why should the author attempt to set forth an order of creation at all? How could he possibly have arrived at the correct order if he was not gifted with a divine revelation? Where else in ancient literature, or in non-Christian literature written before the birth of Geology as a science, is such a successful delineation of the order of creation to be found?

'It is often declared that the second Creation-narrative contradicts the one we have been considering, and certainly it gives an entirely different account of events. But the two narratives are supplementary, not contradictory. The second narrative commences where the first leaves off. It tells in one sentence of the creation of the Heaven and the Earth, omits all reference to the origin of wild plants and animals, and comes at once to a rainless, barren, uncultivated region, where God created man, and planted a garden for him to cultivate.

'One question remains. What appears to be the truth about the creation of animals and plants? Are they all derived from a single ancestor, created by act of God, and gradually moulded by His directing wisdom into the countless forms that have existed in geological time, and that exist today? Or were there a number of new beginnings? Was older living material used, or were the new creations directly "from the dust of the ground?" We submit that on a right understanding of the Creation-narrative in Genesis there is no need for any controversy between science and religion about these questions. If science sets up a godless, materialistic process instead of a Creator, it has to be opposed, but not when it asks or answers such questions as these. No final answer can be given in the present state of our knowledge.

Darwin spoke of the breathing of life into "a few forms, or one". Berg* speaks of tens of thousands of original forms. We have seen that though ancestors can be found in the fossil state for species, genera and families, they are almost invariably missing when we look for some link between the great natural orders – that is to say, creatures that are thoroughly unlike one another. Nor does the argument from embryology prove much as to an animal's ancestry. In the Creation-narrative, the word *bara,* "to create", is not used again and again for every new introduction of life. It is used three times only, for the creation of the heaven and the earth, for the first animal life mentioned, and for man. There is, therefore, abundant room for difference of opinion, both amongst the scientists and amongst the theologians, concerning these questions.

* L. Berg, *Nomogenesis.*

'That which must be firmly held by Christians who honour the Bible as the Word of God is the fact that God is the Creator of the heaven, the earth, and all living things, whatever methods He may have used; that the Creation-narrative of Genesis is a true account; and that man is a special creation of God, though this does not necessarily mean that God created him out of nothing at all.'

International Interest

A.R.S.'s advocacy of Christianity in the universities was not confined to Britain. In 1936 he was invited by the leaders of the Christian student circles in Scandinavia to visit the universities of Oslo, Stockholm, Uppsala and Helsinki. He was accompanied on this journey by Mrs. Rendle Short. He was asked in Stockholm and Helsinki to address meetings of medical men concerning recent advances in British surgery and to attend informal gatherings of the Christian medical societies. The meetings received favourable reports in the daily press. In the student meetings he spoke on such typical subjects as 'Temptation and Victory', 'Prayer', 'Why I believe the Bible to be the Word of God', 'Why I am a Christian', 'On Examinations – and one in Particular'.

The next year, 1937, he was invited to be one of the British speakers to the International Conference of Evangelical Students in Budapest. Other members of medical faculties, such as the late Professor D. M. Blair (Glasgow) and Professor Ferenc Kiss (Budapest) also contributed to the programme. A.R.S. was particularly pleased that twelve senior medical men took part in the communion service at the close of the conference, after which those present remained kneeling in quiet prayer for nearly an hour. The day after the conference, with Professor Ferenc Kiss as interpreter, he addressed a big Christian gathering in one of the main halls of Budapest. He was largely behind the planning of further student international conferences. Who that was present will forget the great international gathering at Cambridge in July 1939 when over a thousand university students from thirty nations came together in conference, with the various delegations brightening the streets with their national costumes?

A Master of Apologetics

A.R.S.'s strength in his appeal to students lay chiefly in his practical application of his extensive general scientific knowledge, particularly in archaeology, Biblical linguistics, biology, geology, and all those subjects which are relevant to an intensive study of the Bible. He remained throughout his life convinced that the theologians had needlessly permitted the Bible to be discredited in the popular mind. They had allowed a false use of scientific investigation to give the appearance that the Bible was mistaken. As his book *Modern Discovery and the Bible* demonstrates, he had a deep, scientifically-held confidence both in the accuracy and also the message of the Bible. He regulated his whole life by it. He saw no incompatibility between the Christian faith and accurately verified scientific knowledge. He was intellectually (as well as emotionally and morally) convinced of the absolute truth of the Christian revelation found in the Bible. To quote his own words – 'The small service I have been seeking to render is to provide demonstration that if we venture to take the Bible at its face value, we shall not need to be hypocrites, pretending to believe what we know to be contrary to facts, nor need we shun all human learning and research as though they were of the devil. The evidence does not compel us. We are not bound, on the other hand, to regard these human achievements as sacrosanct and infallible. Theories come and theories go; old editions of scientific textbooks fetch very small money in the second-hand bookshops. The Bible survives them all.

'Some of the very princes of science have found it possible to be earnest Christians and believers in the Word of God.* We recall with pride Lord Kelvin, the physicist; Dana, the geologist, and even G. J. Romanes, the zoologist, in the evening of his days. One could also mention the names of such eminent men as Sir James Young Simpson, the introducer of chloroform anaesthesia; Lord Lister, the founder of the antiseptic system of surgery; Lord Rayleigh, Sir George Stokes and Clerk Maxwell, the physicists; Professor J. H. Gladstone, Sir William Ramsay and Sir William Perkin, the chemists; Professors James, Boyd Dawkins, Edward Hill, Sir J. Prestwich and Sir J. W. Dawson, to mention only five well-known English geologists, and a very large number of outstanding medical men. There have been scores of modern university men – scholars and scientists – who have faced the problems of recent science, and have nevertheless devoted their spare time, and some of their whole lives, to the preaching of the Gospel.

* There lies in the Bodleian Library at Oxford a confession of faith in 'God's Word written in Holy Scripture' signed by no fewer than 617 members of the British Association for the year 1865.

'Someone may accuse us of intellectual dishonesty in taking up such an attitude; they may imagine that we are trying to hold on to the Bible in the teeth of convincing facts that disprove its authority. That is not a fair deduction. There are no convincing facts that disprove the authority of the Bible. Each may discover for himself more than one possible way in which the inspired narrative squares with the well-accredited observations (I do not say the 'theories') of the scientist. There may be difficulties, and he may not expect that his ideas would be convincing to any but himself. The Bible is full of mysteries that elude our grasp, just as the sciences, and engineering, and medicine, and economics are full of unsolved problems. Happily, there is abundance of light besides. In daily life we do not throw away a whole letter because a word here and there is blurred. If, as we believe, the eternal God of infinite truth and wisdom is at once the Creator and Controller of all material things, and the Author both of Holy Scripture and of 'natural law', then it stands to reason that conflict between science and revelation is an impossibility. God cannot deny Himself. It is we who are short-sighted; our vision of these mysteries is blurred. Thus we think we see conflict where, in fact, there is none.'

A prominent senior member of one of the Universities has described how greatly he was indebted to A.R.S. in his own early years at the university: 'Not only as a speaker to large audiences was he acceptable and popular, but specially when (after supper with his hands under the lapels of his coat and leaning against the mantelpiece) he would invite questions from the audience and deal with each one with clear incisive reasoning. It was at this time that he became most human and most humorous. Many of us will carry a picture of him in this attitude as the most distinctive and most enriching memory of our student years.' For many students these were years of decision which have controlled the subsequent course of their lives. A.R.S. was determined that they should be a time, not of letting slip the Christian faith, but of deepening it and taking a firmer hold of Christ, the one Foundation. That he was effective in doing this was proved by the number of letters received after his death from former students who are now serving Christ in many parts of the world.

CHAPTER 12

The Deeper Fulfilment

*God had only one Son and He was a medical
missionary.*
David Livingstone

Throughout his career A.R.S. was very busy. It is, therefore, important that we should retain a true perspective and ask: What was it that claimed the greatest amount of his free time? There can be little doubt that it was the support of Medical Missions.* He describes for us the early impression made on him by a visit to the Student Missionary Volunteer Movement's Conference at Baslow in late June 1908. It must have been during the summer months between his receiving the Diploma of Tropical Medicine (in April) and his F.R.C.S. (early in June) and the date of his marriage in the December following. The extract is taken from a private note-book, and in a later hand a note is added – 'When this was written, I expected to sail in a month or two to Formosa':

'An early student missionary conference still lives in my mind. What has lived in memory till now is surely worth enshrining in more permanent form. Yet not half of it is capable of being expressed in writing.

'Who can bring back the sense of comradeship with a thousand seeking souls, awaking to new duties, and choosing rather, like Moses, to suffer for Christ's sake than to enjoy "the pleasures of sin for a season"? How recall the sight of their bowed heads and clenched fists, or hear again their earnest conversation? Or see their deep emotion when the speaker, in trembling tones and flashing eyes, spoke of sin, against self, society, and God – "against

* See pages 27–29.

thee, thee only, have I sinned, and done this evil in thy sight". Yet, to the disciples who had fled, the risen Christ condescends to say, "As my Father sent me into the world, even so send I you." And to Peter, who had denied, He first asks "Lovest thou me?", and then commands, "Feed my sheep". The scarcely returned rebel is made an ambassador!

'Of some thirty students who were about to go overseas in missionary service, some spoke. As the first said, "We cannot conquer all our trials by signing the declaration. We cannot put all our hurdles together; they must be jumped one by one, big or small." While we prayed for these volunteers, and while the golden sunset brightened in the west, we sang "For all the saints, who from their labours rest." Will these worthily continue those labours, and enter the apostolic succession? Peter the heroic champion against Sanhedrin and Nero, Paul the builder of the Gentile Church, Polycarp and Justin, martyrs, Origen the mystic and apologist, Tertullian the devoted, the fiery Ambrose, who defied the emperor, Athanasius, alone against the world, Anthony the blessed hermit, Augustine the author of the "Confessions" and the "City of God", Perpetua and Blandina who overcame the sword and flame, Basil, Jerome, Francis of Assisi, Raymond Lull, Francis Xavier, Savonarola, Wycliffe, Tyndale, Luther, Thomas a Kempis, Wesley, Whitefield, Brainerd, Judson, Moffat, Allen Gardiner, Carey, Ian Keith Falconer, George Müller? Will they follow these?'

Beginning of the Missionary Study Movement

As far back as the turn of the century, some young women in Clifton had organized a class for missionary study intended to promote activity which was designed to give assistance to Christian missions and mission hospitals. The first entry in the minute book is: 'Committee Meeting of the Missionary Study Association, held on Tuesday, April 14th 1903. Mrs. Foster announced that she had been considering whether it would not be the right thing to invite young men to join the Association.' Eventually it was unanimously agreed that young men be invited as members! The entry for 12th October records that 'Mrs Foster suggested Mr. Rendle Short's name as Hon. Secretary, but as he will not be free until after Christmas, the Committee decided to go on as we were until then'. Evidently his interest in mission hospitals was already known. Indeed, while still a student he had organized a series of lectures in the Hall of the Blind Asylum (situated where the

University now stands). The speakers were visitors from the Student Missionary Volunteer Union such as Stanley Smith (of 'the Cambridge Seven') and Robert P. Wilder (of the U.S.A.).* Subjects dealt with were 'The Basis of Foreign Missions' and 'The Nature of Non-Christian Religions'.

On 16th January, 1904 A.R.S., who had only recently qualified medically, was welcomed as a member of the Committee. He did not become Secretary, at least in name. Evidence, however, of his thinking and activity immediately appears and continues with almost every subsequent entry. These active young people hired a room in All Saints' Road, and aimed to stir up interest beyond Clifton. Besides their local meetings in Bristol (addressed by returned missionaries or by one of themselves) they proceeded to hold conventions in strategic centres around, such as Yatton, Portbury, Keynsham, Saltford, Shirehampton and Avonmouth.

The classes for missionary study eventually spread among the circles of the Christian Brethren throughout the country, and what became known later as the 'Missionary Study Class Movement' was born. On 28th September, 1910, the Minute Book records 'Dr. Short reported that the Missionary Study Movement had made great headway in Lancashire and Yorkshire, from 25 to 30 Associations having been formed'. In 1910 there was a change of name from 'Missionary Study Association' to 'Missionary Study Class Movement'. By 1912 A.R.S. is found writing to Mr. H. G. Hall, the leader in Lancashire, to Miss Colgrave in Birmingham, and Mr. Lorimer in Buxton, to ask if they would bring contingents from their areas to a residential conference to be organized along the lines of the older Student Volunteer Movement conferences. They agreed. Led by him, the first Missionary Study Class Conference met in Lewisham School, Weston-super-Mare. Few who gathered on that wet Saturday afternoon in August could have guessed the far-reaching consequences of this event.

Miss E. Colgrave in writing of A.R.S's influence on the Movement says:

'Among the Brethren, there were some in authority who were rather narrow-minded and anxious to impose restrictions on these young people. Throughout his life Rendle Short came up

---

* Dr. Robert P. Wilder of Princeton toured in Europe (1881–1914) as the head of the highly successful movement – the Student Volunteer Movement for Foreign Missions – of which he was one of the chief founders.

against these things, but such was his love of peace and hatred of division that he submitted willingly. Even when these limitations were imposed by men who failed to recognize his mental and spiritual gifts, he bore no malice. Happily there were very many, even in his young days, who were out to give him all the support they could.

'In 1907 there were five classes, but by 1912 when the first M.S.C. Conference was held at Weston the number had risen to sixty. It must be remembered that Rendle Short was entirely responsible for planning and carrying out this first conference. There was no committee. There were some sixty conference members, most of them very young. Rendle Short was among the oldest, although he was only thirty-two.

'He himself gave the opening address. "This conference", he said, "is the first of its kind. I think that its meaning and purpose is to be found in St. Paul's words: 'Say to Archippus, Take heed to the ministry which thou has received in the Lord, that thou fulfil it.'* I feel I should like to say to each one by name: 'Take heed to the ministry which thou hast received'. This conference is a crisis of opportunity for each one of us – firstly, because there has been so much prayer for it. Not in England alone but in Europe, in India and around the camp fires of Africa they are praying for each one of you. Then it is a crisis of opportunity because God has shown His hand so plainly in the preparation. Five great mountains of difficulty have been removed which seemed to threaten its existence. Lastly, it is a crisis of opportunity because most of you are just at an age when you are led to your life's work. Fulfil your ministry."

'What is that ministry? It may be that some of us are needed abroad. Others perhaps are needed to stay at home. For those it is necessary that they should try to uphold the work abroad by their zeal, their prayers, their interest. If you were to die, would you be missed in the foreign field?'

Miss Colgrave continues: 'The impression made by that address has lasted over the forty years that have elapsed since it was given. He addressed the conference again on the Wednesday following. He told very briefly the stories of A. N. Groves, Count Guicciardini, T. P. Rossetti, Matamoros of Spain, Leonard Strong and John Rhymer. This first "Weston" conference made an im-

* Col. 4:17.

mense impression on all those present. It resulted in Rendle Short's becoming more widely known as a speaker and as one with his own message for thinking people.

'At the 1913 Conference, the numbers were doubled. Extra schools had to be taken for the 120 members. Throughout the year 1913 Rendle Short was drivingly busy. His wife wrote to a friend: "I have never known him so busy. I see less and less of him; and he tells me that soon I shall see even less. Cheerful, isn't it?"

'The 1914 Conference was planned to follow the same lines as the previous two, with the difference that Rendle Short was to give an address on "The Christian's attitude to the political problems of the day". Thirty-six hours after the Conference gathered, war with Germany was declared. By the time he returned from France other men had begun to shoulder the responsibility of the M.S.C. conferences, and they sprang up in various parts of the country. In 1920 there were no fewer than six, and he was a speaker at five of them.

'At the 1920 Bournemouth Conference Rendle Short gave an address on "The Christian's Armour" emphasising "If you are to be a missionary you must *earn* the greatest honour this world affords by character-culture, Bible study, education and commendation from those who know you." In the years 1921 to 1931 there were never fewer than four annual M.S.C. conferences. Rendle Short was a speaker at an average of three a year. A "Coming of Age" Conference took place at Malvern in 1933, when he contributed three of the addresses.'

Finding New Missionary Doctors

Many examples could be given of A.R.S's unobtrusive method of bringing the missionary call before young people. Throughout his life he found a considerable number of qualified doctors for overseas posts. One of these writes:

'Dr. –, being ill, had sent a telegram from overseas asking him to find a Christian locum for him as soon as possible. A few days later Mr. Short was in Birmingham on professional work. He was writing in a café near the station, characteristically using his time purposefully until the arrival of the return train to Bristol. Meantime, overhead a vivid thunderstorm had come on. I was on my motor cycle in the deluge and with water in the carburetter, the engine shut down right outside the restaurant. I walked into it for shelter. He at once spotted me as I came in through the door, called me over and told me of the need. He suggested, with dry humour, that divine guidance had led me, water-logged as I was, into that café, so that he could talk things over with me! I was overseas in that place within a few weeks and he always followed the work there with keen interest and prayerful suggestions.'

Another missionary writes:

'It was at one of the Monday evening prayer meetings in his home, when A.R.S. gave an account of a recent holiday in North Africa, that I was first interested to go there in missionary service. He told how he had spent the time in visiting different mission stations. His clear descriptions made me realize my responsibility in the matter. He told me, too, to go to the instrument department of Ferris and Company and choose the surgical instruments I needed and added that he would settle the account.'

There was a very shrewd and realistic streak in his approach to the problem of divine guidance. He did not believe in accepting a new volunteer too easily. He certainly never encouraged any young man or woman to embark lightly on a missionary future. He would also continue to give much wise counsel when they were overseas, particularly to the medical workers. A woman surgeon, now in India, relates her experience of his robust common sense:

'I was at a crisis of difficult choices in my life. Four days previously I had been suddenly precipitated into this by receiving the scarcely anticipated news that I had succeeded in the exams for the F.R.C.S.Ed. In a most unexpected way I met Professor Rendle Short and told him of my dilemma and that I had now clearly come to a cross-roads where I must discern God's will for my future. Professor Short took me aside and for about half an hour shot out a series of the most searching questions. I felt that my whole character was being laid absolutely bare. There was no deceiving this penetrating mind. Not only did he scan my medical abilities, he also searched my spiritual experiences and stability, in a way that few friends would have dared to do. Finally he asked my age. When I replied, his face changed. The apparent severity and sternness suddenly melted. He beamed and in a gentle voice of true admiration he commented "You must be about the youngest ever to have obtained the Fellowship"!

'He then gave me a masterly analysis of the various places in the mission fields of the world where the training that I had received would be of most value. He put the emphasis on what certainly would now seem to have been the place to which God had purposed for me to go. He completely unbent in the latter part of this talk. Thereafter my impression of him was not that of a severe intellectual, but of a very kind and true friend, of inestimable value. Some months later, he prayed for me at a meeting where friends were bidding farewell before I sailed for India. His prayer – "Lord make her acceptable to the people of India" – will always live in my memory. He seemed to understand completely the task I was about to undertake.'

His unobtrusive way of helping is well illustrated by another letter: 'When I had recently qualified, was holding resident posts at the Bristol General Hospital, and expecting soon to go out to Africa, A.R.S. was always very kind to me. He was particularly interested in my intention to become a medical missionary. Not long after I had started work at Bristol, he asked me if I intended to take a course in Tropical Medicine. I said: "No, I have only just qualified and I hope to go out to Africa next autumn. I do not see how I can fit in several months for a tropical course." Then he said, in his slow, deliberate way: "I myself took the full course in Tropical Medicine a few years ago. If you can come to my home every Tuesday evening for an hour I will take you through my notes on the course. It will not, of course, be as good as the real thing, but it will be a lot better than nothing." That was how I came to take my first Tropical Medicine course. It was the most thorough and interesting that I have ever subsequently received!'

Writing in the Cause of Missions

In the early records of the Missionary Study Association of Bristol, there is a minute dated 21st November, 1905: 'Dr. Short proposed that the Missionary Study Association should publish a small booklet containing some account of the missionaries gone out from the assemblies in Bristol. It should contain photos. For guidance as to the information wanted about their work, a model letter should be sent to certain missionaries.' This resulted in a pamphlet published in 1907, entitled *Our Missionaries*. The further result, however, was the appearance of a more elaborate book from his pen entitled *A Modern Experiment in Apostolic Missions*. This contains a wealth of information about missionaries in all quarters of the globe whose work had previously been very little known, and it became the text-book of the Missionary Study Classes.

The Witness of June 1938 carries an article by A.R.S. which is simply entitled 'Medical Work'. Five reasons are given why everyone should help medical missions. He writes: 'I submit to you the following reasons why we should believe in medical missions:

1. The pattern and example of our Lord Jesus Christ.
2. The work of caring for the sick and preaching the gospel is a sound Christian tradition.
3. The bodily needs of the developing countries cry out for help.
4. This form of service opens many doors that are otherwise very hard to push.
5. If a number of our brothers and sisters are going out to the remote parts hundreds, even thousands, of miles from the nearest European doctor or hospital; it is surely only right and proper that someone with a certain amount of medical skill should go with them.'

He also was concerned with prayer for missions, a subject which he approached in his usual methodical manner, recommending: 'A good method is to draw up a monthly time-table. Let the first day be for some general intercession, the second for candidates in training, the third for financial help, the fourth for Christian workers holding the ropes at home, the fifth for the Jews, the sixth for the neglected counties of the British Isles, the seventh for France, the eighth for Spain and Portugal, and so on. Thus, by degrees we get all round the world. In so doing it will be possible to ask for much for all the missionaries whom we know without forgetfulness or weariness or lack of attention. After a few months we shall remember the list so well that we shall not even need to refer to it. We shall say instinctively, 'Let me see: it was China yesterday; Japan today.'

His prayers, however, always issued in practical deeds. Any Bristol doctor or nurse was going abroad in Christian service could always rely upon being told to go to a well-known instrument maker and choose what instruments were specially needed. The bill was to be sent to him.

Visit to North Africa

Considering his interest in countries overseas, he travelled abroad on very few occasions. Towards the close of his career, however, and as a twenty-first birthday present to his eldest daughter, he arranged a visit to North Africa. At last he had a chance to see personally the type of missionary work which he had studied and supported all his professional life. As one would expect, his account is typically stimulating:

'The word had gone round that a "proper" surgeon had come out from England, so on that Good Friday patients gathered in from far and near. There were scores of them. Many were simple and commonplace; some were very much out of the ordinary, and I had never seen or read of the like. There were horrible deep ulcers of the neck, perhaps tuberculous in half-starved people with no resistance to the disease, perhaps gummata. There was one old chap, who had walked ten miles, with the tip of his finger swollen to the size of a plum, and the bone replaced by a bag of whitish jelly. It may have been a degenerated chondroma. It was so much in his way that we amputated the last phalanx under a local anaesthetic. He started out quite happily on the long walk home. Towards dusk, I was asked to go and see a man who had gone off his head and was violent. I found him sitting in a dark hut, with a dozen men of the tribe squatting round him. There was not much we could do, but I had a bottle of ammonium bromide which we had brought for seasickness, and I suggested that they gave him doses from that. (We missed that bromide horribly on the homeward trip.) I hope it gave him and the rest of them some sleep.

'We found it a very great advantage to be escorted by the missionaries. They were able to take us into native homes. In the native quarter of Algiers, we came across a quack doctor ready to do dry cupping. He had a lancet, a glass cup, and some paper to burn to exhaust the air in the cup. I tried to buy the whole kit for my students, but he asked such a preposterous price that I turned away. It was a pity. My surgery class would have loved it.'

CHAPTER 13

The Shaftesbury Men's Club

*'Keep in harmony with one another; instead of
being ambitious, associate with humble folk;
never be conceited.'*

St. Paul

Shortly after the death of A.R.S. in October 1953, the
following appeared in the *Redland Park Recorder:* 'The members
of the Thursday night men's Bible School at the Shaftesbury
Institute have lost their well loved Leader. For forty years Dr. A.
Rendle Short has been in constant touch with this gathering. In
1935 a photo was taken on the lawn of the Dings' House. Since
that date thirty-one of our men have passed away; and now our
beloved Leader has gone to his eternal reward. The loss to us can
never be measured; he was always delighted to be with us. Even
after a strenuous day he would expound the Scriptures to us in a
wonderful way. He never refused to visit a sick or aged member,
however busy or tired he might be.' This simple statement
epitomises the outcome of what A.R.S. himself regarded as the
most fruitful piece of work he had done as a lay preacher. For a
member of the medical profession it is one which must be almost
unique.

The Life of Faith (1st June, 1938) described this men's class
as it was between the two World Wars:

The Shaftesbury Workmen's Institute

'In the neighbourhood of Temple Meads Station, Bristol, is
an area which has been for many years the scene of an active mission work conducted by what is known as the Shaftesbury
Crusade. In 1912 Dr. A. Rendle Short, the well-known surgeon
and later Professor at Bristol University, was asked to take charge

of a class for working men. The class grew strikingly under his leadership, and expanded into a Bible school which has now some seventy members and a weekly attendance of from forty to fifty. Dr. Short probably conducts the school thirty weeks in the year, visiting speakers being secured upon the other occasions. When he was on service abroad for eight months during the Great War, the men, or such of them as were available, kept things going loyally and efficiently. The membership is drawn from the humbler toilers of the district and from the ranks of the unemployed. Many of the men are in that pathetically unfortunate class, the casual workers and those who find the search for work hopeless by reason of their age. They love the fellowship of this weekly gathering and support it with a strong and even touching fidelity. It is one of the best *bona fide* working-class groups I have met.

'The method is simplicity itself. There is hymn-singing, prayer, Bible reading, and exposition. Dr. Short's manner is informal and conversational. He sits at the table, pocket Bible open before him, and talks in a quiet, easy fashion. Questions and discussion are freely and frankly encouraged, and honest opinions are candidly expressed. There is no restriction as to attendance, and some among the habitués entertain pronounced views on matters affecting the general life of the community. They have no need to hesitate in the utterance of their conviction for fear these should run counter to the mind of leader or fellow-member.

'Dr. Short's practice is to take a book of the Bible, or the life of one of its notable characters, and devote several evenings to a short course of studies upon the subject. From time to time he varies this with two or three nights given to more general themes. He confesses an amazement at the way in which the men receive with avidity expositions of books which it might not have been supposed would interest them. He instanced the First Epistle of Peter as an example. . . .'

What was Involved

To any reader who may be unfamiliar with what is called for in such activities, a further explanation may be necessary. If they are to provide a real home for the older men, they demand in the leader sincerity, true humility of spirit, a generous understanding of human nature, and a sense of humour. To the surprise of many of his colleagues, the hurrying, ruthlessly efficient surgeon of the Royal Infirmary proved more than adequate at each point. He obviously enjoyed leading this men's meeting and visiting the members in their own homes. He would often tell with obvious relish the story of the member of the class who prayed the same prayer each week. It contained a phrase which no doubt would be very good medicine for those who pride themselves on their public speaking or preaching. 'Oh, God, we thank you for the Doctor and his message to us, *given in great weakness.*'(!)

The following was derived from an interview with the City Missioner, Mr. E. Bale, who for nearly forty years assisted A.R.S. in this work:

'Dr. Short used to say to me, "This men's class is the most successful Christian work I ever do. If God were to call me to whole-time Christian teaching and work, I would devote my life to the work here at Shaftesbury." The Class commenced at 7 p.m. on a Thursday and closed at 8.30 p.m. After the talk, the men would ask questions. Whatever the subject might be, and however interested the men clearly seemed to be, the Doctor always insisted on closing promptly. At times when he came, he would look quite exhausted. Sometimes he would 'phone from Cheddar, Aust, Wells, and elsewhere, to let us know he was coming a little late, or if it was quite impossible for him to get to the class, which was not often. Every year he would regularly go with the men on their summer outing to Minehead.

'Just before the end of the last session (1953 – the year of Rendle Short's death) – I asked him if he would care to visit one of the men who was ill. He agreed. As the man lived near the Shaftesbury, we walked to the house. A message had been taken on to tell the sick man's wife that we were coming so that she could clear up a bit. This man had only recently joined the Bible School and previously he had not gone to any place of worship. After a brief talk, Dr. Short brought out his Bible and read, then knelt down and prayed. After we had gone the wife said, "Harry, there's something wrong here; we have never before had anything like this in our home." There is later evidence that they both became Christians.

Stories from the Shaftesbury

'Each week the Doctor would take for his talks such subjects as the life of Moses, Joshua, Elijah, etc. One evening Joe X. asked if he would take the book of Jonah. Dr. Rendle Short was rather surprised at this and asked why he particularly wanted

Jonah's life story. Joe looked up and said, "Well, it's like this, sir, I shan't be here much longer – I'm going Home soon, and when I get up yonder Jonah will say to me, 'Well, Joe, what did Dr. Short say about me down under?' Then I shall be bound to say, 'Oh, he didn't mention you, sir'." With a twinkle in his eye Dr. Short at once agreed that this matter should be put right, and so he took the book of Jonah for the three weeks following.' Joe died some five weeks later.

'One evening a somewhat wild looking man came in, and asked "Is this the place where Dr. Short holds his meetings?" "Yes", I said. "Can anyone come?" "Yes, we shall be very pleased to welcome you." He added that he was an atheist and that he knew nothing about Christianity. When the Doctor arrived I told him that this new man was present. The man listened intently and came again and continued coming. Soon there was a considerable change in his manner. Later on he asked if he could have his own Bible. When one of our members was taken seriously ill with cancer, this same man visited him repeatedly and asked "Is there anything I can do to show my love for you?" It then became known that he was a taxi driver, and the sick man asked if he could be taken out for a drive, which was gladly arranged. Although he found words difficult this man continued to speak eloquently in deeds.'

One of the City Missioner's stories which most gave pleasure to A.R.S. runs as follows: 'There was a man in the district who used to sell medical powders to cure hangovers. His trade was done chiefly on Sunday mornings. He began to come to the Shaftesbury. He really loved the Doctor and came more and more under his influence. At length he professed to have become a Christian, and the neighbours began to take out £5 bets that it wouldn't last a month. Until then his little shop had always opened on Sundays. But now in the window a card would regularly appear: "Closed on Sunday. The Sabbath well spent brings a week of content." One day, I received a note, asking me to go to see the wife. She at once asked "What have you been doing to our old man up there at the Shaftesbury?" "Well, it won't last; of course it won't. You don't know father like I do. Do you know that he has cursed me every morning for thirty years? He has never given me any money for a new dress or clothes. I have had to work for everything. It won't last; it can't." I left her, saying I would come to see her again later. "It will be all over in a month", she called after me. A little later, another note reached me, marked "Urgent" this time. I went up promptly. She said "It's still going on, you know! Do you know what happened this morning?" "No." "He actually brought me up a cup of tea! So I said, 'Don't be so soft!' and he replied: 'There you are, my dear' – instead of his oaths and curses.' 'What on earth has come over you?' I asked him. All he said was 'It's because I love God, and I want to show it and make up for the past'."

'It was his wife's birthday the next day, and the two sons were already talking about what to expect. They said to each other, "Now you will see what father's Christianity is like; this is the testing point. He won't think of her birthday – he hasn't enough brains for that." When they came down the next morning, two plates stood one on top of the other on the table, on them had been placed a little piece of paper. (Incidentally, it had taken him more than half-an-hour to write the inscription, for he had only learnt to read and write after he was sixty.) It ran "Dear Sally, with Christian love". Underneath the plate were two pound notes. When the boys came home, the mother said, "Look what father left". The reply was "Yes, but that's only your wages – there will be nothing next Friday". Friday came. The boys watched. Father paid his wages down! This was one of the greatest triumphs that Dr. Short had at the Shaftesbury.

'All the time this man had been working at the brewery, where earlier his friends had regularly made him drunk. He would now sit at the Bible Class proud of his reading glass. It had been given to him by Dr. Short. He wouldn't let anyone else touch it. He had initially learnt to read from the Bible.

Home Visits

'Dr. Short was also fond of visiting the men in their homes. When he was very busy, however, I did not like to ask him to do much. But at other times we have been into six or more homes during a single night. He would sit down with the men and talk to them as man to man, no matter what were the conditions in the homes. Sometimes we could see the sky through the ceiling. He was very liberal and helped me to keep a fund in order unobtrusively to assist the deserving.

'Late one evening I said to Dr. Short, "There is a member who wants to see you. Can you spare a few minutes?" He replied that he could. The man we went to see had been quietly attending the Shaftesbury for several years. He was obviously very ill. The Doctor greeted him, and asked whether he had anything he wished to talk about. "This, doctor," he said, "who shall ascend into the hill of the Lord? or who shall stand in His holy place? He that hath clean hands, and a pure heart; who hath not lifted up his soul unto vanity."* Doctor, by the grace of God I have come to believe!" On this occasion, Dr. Short was so overcome by emotion that on the way back he didn't speak.

'Then there was the battered old prize fighter, nicknamed *Punch*(!) Dr. Short and I went to see him several times. At last he received Christ. I visited him just before the end. He asked me to read Psalm 23 and pray. "Why?" I asked. "Because soon I shall be in the presence of the Lord. I shall tell Him how much Dr. Short and you have meant in my salvation."

'One day I said to Dr. Short, "I wish you would go to see old —. No one lives with him now because of his foul language. His wife has left him." We went. The man told us that no one had called to see him for over forty years. We asked him whether he would like to be reconciled to his wife. Eventually she was found and they were together again. He began to attend the Bible Class and came to love Dr. Short. About a fortnight after joining he asked if he could have a Bible. One with large print was obtained for him. Soon after, coming down Cheese Lane, I saw him reading his Bible with a little boy sitting on his knee!

'On another occasion I asked Dr. Short if he would visit a man who had been attending the Shaftesbury and who was ill. As soon as he arrived he said: "I am sorry you are like this, my friend, we will tell the Lord about it". He knelt on the stone floor in the poor, badly ventilated room, and prayed such a prayer as I have seldom heard. Having seen Dr. Short off in his car I came back to the house. The man asked me: "What do you think about a doctor like that, kneeling next to a man like me down here? If he knew what I was like he wouldn't talk to me. Thank God for such men? It's the first prayer that has ever been prayed in this home."

One night a policeman said to me: "Well now, look, I am not a Christian. But if you people can get hold of men such as you have here tonight, all we can say is that we thank God for this men's meeting. You save us a host of trouble. When we are on duty here we often stand under the window and listen to the singing." '

* This verse had served as the text from which Rendle Short had earlier given an address on justification by faith.

CHAPTER 14

The End of the Road

*'One of the blessed concomitants of this
remarkable faith is that it places me in a new
and far higher relationship to my family, my
friends and my Creator, and genders a deeper
interest in, and tenderness for, all men.'*
Howard Kelly

The approach of the year at which a professor of the University, or Surgeon at the Infirmary, would be due to retire found A.R.S. full of undiminished powers. His physical stamina and his love of teaching were unabated. His pen continued to work assiduously and he retained his co-editorship of the *Medical Annual* until his actual retirement from public duty. It so happened that shortage of staff during the 1939–1945 War meant that he remained on several years beyond the official date.

Finally, in 1946, he became Professor of Surgery Emeritus. He then took up, as a retirement task, a piece of research following up his earlier interest in the geographic distribution of malignant disease in the South West. This involved keeping a register of all reported deaths due to the types of malignant disease which were included in the survey. It also required further investigation where the original information was inadequate or special interest was attracted by any particular features. He gave a lot of time and care to this work and it was continued by Professor R. Milnes-Walker, his successor as Professor of Surgery.

On his last teaching round in 1946 at the Infirmary, as is the custom, almost all the staff turned up to show their appreciation of his ability and personality. He seemed as active and as energetic and as buoyant as ever as he left the Infirmary that afternoon to start on the years which for most men are called retirement, but which found him creating new fields for his initiative and industry.

There was a touch of irony in the circumstance that the war had caused him to retire several years after he had reached the age-limit* for surgeons. For he had on one memorable occasion strongly advised a group of students to be sure that when they grew old they did not outstay their welcome. He emphasized the point by describing a letter which he had written when he was thirty years old. It was entitled 'A.R.S. Young to A.R.S. Old'. In it he solemnly gave himself advice on how to avoid the foibles of men over the normal retiring age. He ended the letter by warning himself on becoming 'sixty-five' promptly to retire and to let younger men take over the appointments. It was a step which, when it came to the point, he did not find so easy to take.

Persisting Traits

Registrars and housemen at the Infirmary during his final years were impressed by the way in which he kept up to the end certain of his attitudes and personal customs. For example, in his life-long anxiety not to lose a passing moment there was a constant risk that he would appear busy to the point of abruptness. He was undoubtedly aware of this and seemed not to be quite so concerned about it in the case of his private patients! But his attitude in the wards of the Infirmary was very different. The more in need a patient was the more his true self would be seen. If he had been rather off-hand and brief with a patient, on suddenly recollecting the fact, he would turn round and go back two or three beds, and give a more careful and kindly explanation of the position than a moment before he had bothered to make sufficiently clear. One practice which particularly was noted by his registrars, was often shyly performed to the point of embarrassment. If there had been a death in any of his wards, he would sit down at the end of the ward round and write a personal letter to the nearest relative.

This anxiety to put to good use every fleeting moment was, of course, seen most particularly in his home and in his spiritual interests. It was the secret of the amount that got done outside of his main task of surgery. The housekeeper commented that in a period of service which had lasted over thirty years she had never gone into the drawing-room or study and found Mr. Short idling. He was always sitting up occupied in reading, study, writing or making

* The age of retirement under the N.H.S. regulations is 65 years.

notes. Perhaps there could have been no greater testimony to his use of every minute.

With some ease he could read in French, German, Old Testament Hebrew and New Testament Greek. He was never, however, a linguist as such and contented himself with reading in the languages in which he was interested. Having taught himself to read Hebrew he would frequently use the quiet of a Sunday afternoon to study the Hebrew Old Testament – sometimes sitting with a scroll across his lap.

The Ceaseless Letter-Writer

This capacity in the economy of time also enabled him to employ to the full his fruitful powers of advising by post the many students and others who wrote to him. He was particularly concerned to assist any in intellectual difficulties. The following is an example of one of his letters. It was written to a student in a College of Education, who meeting for the first time what in theological circles is known as 'the Kenosis Theory', had written concerning the extent of Christ's knowledge during the period of his human life:

'I deeply sympathize with your struggles to believe in spite of difficulties, and pray that you may come through to a happy faith. I am not going to answer all your questions in this letter. Some can wait for another time. Here I concentrate on two or three points of importance. First, we cannot by searching find out God. All science, all knowledge, has a central well-explored region, and a frontier beyond which we cannot see, and may never be able to see. Where knowledge and reason end, faith begins. God lies beyond that frontier. He does not choose to show us so much of Himself that it is intellectually impossible to disbelieve. He wants our free choices, not our dragooned intellects. The agnostic scientist can always say: "I have an alternative explanation, which I prefer." As R. E. D. Clark has shown in his *Scientific Rationalism and Christian Faith* and in his *Darwinism: Before and After,* there are psychological reasons why well-known agnostic scientists will accept *any* theory rather than believe in God.

'In both your letters you write about your struggles to believe in God, but you do not mention Jesus Christ. Before He came, belief in God stood by itself, and does so still in heathen countries. But where the New Testament is available and He is

therefore known as a Father, a new and living way has been opened to God. "No man cometh to the Father but by me." "Neither
knoweth any man the Father, but the Son, and he to whomsoever
the Son will reveal him" (see Heb. 10:19, 20; John 14:6, 8, 9; Mat.
11:27–30; Heb. 1:1–3). I often think of a doctor, a consultant,
known not to me but to a relative of mine, who was earnestly seeking God and wanted to talk all the time with her about his search.
Yet he had no use for Jesus Christ. So he found nothing, and I will
not distress you by pursuing his story to the end. Such a pity! Why
could he not take God's road, instead of trying to climb some as-
cent of his own?

'You say that your greatest difficulty is that three and a half
years of prayer have evoked no response. Probably there has been
more response than you think. You might have given up all hope
and desire to find Him and been sunk. Maybe it will comfort you to
read the story of Mr. Fearing in *Pilgrim's Progress* and John
Bunyan's remarks about him after he had gone over the river.
Please think about this letter and write again.'

Devotional Life

As we would expect, the robust Christian life of A.R.S. was
based on a regular daily practice of prayer. Every morning after
breakfast he would take the family 'reading', in which he would
read a few verses of Holy Scripture and offer a brief prayer. Again,
late at night, he would pray with Mrs. Short. When the house
began to grow still with the retirement of the younger people, he
would relax and read a little in some form of devotional literature.
He would then study the Bible or prepare sermons and addresses.
He rarely went to bed before midnight.

Few professional men have managed regularly to pack so
much of a varied nature into a day as A.R.S. contrived to do
throughout his whole career. We have his own description of the
sort of life he led:

'The combination of Surgery and preaching can lead to
difficult situations. Surgical cases are often very urgent indeed,
night and day one has to respond to a call, it may be fifty miles
away, though less often today than formerly. Operations cannot be
finished to time; there may be a late start, or unforeseen difficulties
may cause delays. Throughout my active surgical life I have
always preached two or three times a week, at least. Here is the

programme for a couple of weeks in 1946, omitting consultations and operations for private patients, visiting at nursing homes, and hospital ward rounds, all of which take up a good deal of time. And it was after I had retired from university teaching and from my main hospital.

Nov. 17 (Sun.) Preaching service in evening.
„ 18 Prayer meeting.
„ 19 Two committees and a lecture in the evening.
„ 20 Visited a Gloucester hospital. Meeting in the evening.
„ 21 Addressed a meeting and attended committee in evening.
„ 22 Preached to German P.O.W.s at a country camp in evening.
„ 23 Preached in evening.
„ 24 Addressed three meetings.
„ 25 Addressed meeting for medical students at Cambridge.
„ 26 Preached in Bristol.
„ 27 Addressed British Medical Association meeting at Yeovil (the car was held up by floods on the way).
„ 28 Meeting in the evening.
„ 29 Addressed meeting in evening.
„ 30 Business meeting.
Dec. 1 (Sun.) Free day.
Preached at Newport.

'Only some three or four times, in the course of many years, a messenger has walked up the aisle to demand a quick end to the sermon and a hasty departure. But it is wonderful how seldom there has been an absolute *impasse,* so that the preacher failed to turn up and could give no notice. This has not happened oftener than three or four times in forty years. Occasionally, I am ashamed to say, a meeting has slipped the memory, from faulty booking, or from failing to look at the book.

'I repeat, the combination of hospital and private surgical practice, instruction of medical students and post-graduates, attendance on the innumerable committees. that a position on a university senate necessitates, with preaching near to home or far away, does not leave much leisure for other things. But I cannot think of any other way of life that I could have preferred to live. It would have been absolutely impossible without two of the major blessings of Providence, good health and the devoted care, first of my mother, and then of my wife.'

The Heart of It All

Many of his friends among the Brethren have always thought that he was at his best when speaking at a celebration of the Lord's Supper. At such times he revealed a spirit which goes to the very heart of the devotional life of the church. His brief expositions and homilies were packed full of the deepest insight into the meaning of Holy Scripture and the vicissitudes of everyday Christian experience. The members of the regular congregations were unconsciously imbibing almost a complete theological course. Yet blended with the theory was a strong and practical challenge. An unexpected feature of some of his public prayers was that he would use (in what were extempore prayers) collects memorized from the prayer Book of the Church of England. One Sunday morning at Bethesda he had used such a prayer from the Anglican Communion Service. As the members of the congregation were leaving an elderly member, who vigorously held that 'written prayers' were wrong, was heard to remark to his neighbour: 'Mr. Short prayed very beautifully this morning. At times he sounded inspired.'

His was a perfect illustration of what is meant by defining preaching as 'the truth expressed through personality'. He inherited from his father an excellent, strong and clear voice. His delivery was slow and measured. He was free from mannerisms. He preferred good robust Anglo-Saxon monosyllables which tended to warm the heart and nerve the arm. The Authorized Version of the Bible and Bunyan controlled his word choices. (Visitors of Germanic origin could easily follow and understand him because he spoke in an English which was nearer to their own languages. Those of Latin stock had more difficulty.) He would carefully demonstrate his main thesis and then deftly introduce a poem or verse of a hymn to drive home his point. Finally would come the almost sudden ending, leaving the hearer somewhat surprised but strongly stimulated to improve on his own spiritual attainment! Typical of these long remembered endings is the following, culled from Bunyan: ' "Then," said the guide, "why did you not cry that some might have come for your succour?" Valiant for Truth: "So I did, to my King, Who I knew could hear and afford invisible help and that was sufficient for me!" '

He might also end a sermon thus: 'But may we pray to be delivered from the cross? I don't know. Can we be Christians and shirk the cross? I don't know. That is a door on which it is useless to knock. Does the road wind uphill all the way? Yes to the very end.' On other occasions he would close with a remark such as 'We must not pray "Lead us not into temptation" when our own legs take us there . . .!' About the basic necessity for faith in Christ he could be very outspoken. On one occasion he closed an address on the 'Book of Life' by quietly remarking: 'I solemnly declare that the rites of no church on earth will save you apart from the saving grace of God accompanying and transcending them. Those whose names are not "written in the Lamb's book of Life" will, at the last Great Assize, be cast from Him. I'll say no more about it; but it is in the Book.'

Closeness to the Family

Retirement gave A.R.S. more time to enjoy his family, his grandchildren and much else that gave him pleasure. It would, however, be a great mistake to suppose that – in spite of his busy life – he was not throughout a thoughtful parent with a strong love for his home and family. In spite of all his other activities, as the three children were growing up, he was mindful of their developing needs, and at the week-ends or on holidays could be the best and most interesting of companions. Members of the family and his nephews are unanimous concerning the interest and mirth he contributed to the holiday parties by his inventiveness and dry humour. Since these chapters have been chiefly concerned with A.R.S.'s professional and spiritual life, it is time to add some reference to this other side of his life.

As earlier pages have made clear, he was loyally supported in their early crisis and change of plans by Mrs. Rendle Short. She had trained as a nurse and came from a similar religious and cultural background. From the first, he had frankly discussed his outlook and ambitions so she knew what she was in for! Some of the ways in which she adapted to ever more strenuous demands have already been mentioned. Soon after her engagement, she was walking in Clifton when one of the Chiefs from the Royal Infirmary crossed the road and accosted her with 'Oh! I understand that you are the lady who is going to marry the Encyclopaedia Britannica'. At times she must have thought that she had done so.

Mrs. Rendle Short's own capacity for industry was not far behind that of A.R.S. and was invaluable throughout his career. She helped him in a variety of ways, answering the telephone, making engagements, taking care of his instruments, indexing books, and routine checking of material for his medical and surgical writings. Similarly, in the work of the Missionary Study Conferences she was as active as he. Her ability in speaking at women's meetings caused her to be in great demand, nor was she far behind him in devotion and active support of the Shaftesbury Crusade. Her understanding and support must have been quite invaluable in the early days when professional work and Christian witness were carried on in circumstances of considerable financial difficulty. During the year 1910 he noted: 'We can only be sure of £50 this year.' The sentiment expressed by his wife when later she looked back on these days was 'Thank God for every day of it. It gives one the power of infinite sympathy'.

Soon after the time of his retirement, the health of Mrs. Rendle Short began to deteriorate. In 1951 she became seriously ill and afterwards remained a partial invalid. Towards the end of her life, her movements were further restricted through a gradual loss of sight. Throughout these difficult days A.R.S. was active in support and in his share of the work in the home.

The elder daughter, Coralie,* has many happy memories of companionship and outings; and also of their many discussions of some of his favourite periods in history. 'Then there were the country walks. He took me for walks as far back as I can remember; he loved the country. He taught me many things about birds and fossils. Then I used often to ride on the step of his bicycle, one foot on the little bar at the back, one knee on the carrier. We went for miles and miles like that, often setting out on Sunday afternoons to visit the little country meetings and chapels round Bristol of which he was so fond. If it was wet he wore leggings and had a big mackintosh cape and always his grey trilby hat. I think he enjoyed these times as much as I did, because he wrote in 1949, when I went abroad: "You have been a very dear daughter to me, always, since we took our walks together when you were a very little girl

---

* Coralie Rendle Short, Ch.M., F.R.C.O.G. formerly Professor of Gynaecology in the University of East Africa, Kampala and later, at the Haile Selassie I University, Addis Ababa, Ethiopia.

asking innumerable questions, over and over again."

'How many other people's questions he must have answered in his life! The point was he always knew the answer. He could always tell you like a shot the foreign policy of some minister of Henry VIII, or any other question set for homework at school. When I was ten he bought me a bicycle and taught me to ride. Then we would ride together, often leaving our bikes chained up and walking part of the way. He loved particularly walking along hill tops such as Crook's Peal.'

A.R.S.'s younger daughter Morwenna* has an equal store of intriguing stories of her father. 'When we were ill, both as children and when grown up, he would come and read to us from *Just So Stories* or Sherlock Holmes, his favourite being "The Cat that Walked by Itself" and "The Elephant's Child". The latter was particularly suitable because the flowing Victorian English was his own language. When speaking, he never hesitated or used indefinite terms, or slang, or colloquialisms. He also read *The Seven Pillars of Wisdom* to us, and John Buchan's books, and poetry – particularly narrative verse. We always much enjoyed it.

'His ability for imparting knowledge was quite incredible. Once told something by him it was never forgotten. Once something was explained it was really understood. What can I say more? This, perhaps, that I never asked him a single question on any subject, all my life, to which he did not know the answer. No doubt other people found the same. Certainly streams of people were always coming to the house for advice on the most extraordinary subjects.'

His son, John,† who also followed his father in a medical career, confirms these tributes to the warmth of affection of their father and the many ways in which he contributed to the more informal sides of their upbringing and education. 'He wrote once a week to the children. He always worked very hard in the train; indeed a train journey was the main time when he did his writing. He was a firm believer in every member of the family paying their own way. If he lent them money, it was always at a recognized rate of interest. In this way he taught us the value of money.

---

* Morwenna Rendle Short, S.R.N., S.C.M., trained at St. Thomas's Hospital as a nursing Sister.

† Tyndale John Rendle Short, MA., M.D., F.R.C.P., D.C.H., Professor of Paediatrics, University of Brisbane, Queensland.

'He did not press his advice on his own family except on most exceptional occasions. This was one principle he observed throughout his life. Indeed, he would never give advice unless it was asked for.'

He made friends easily with small children by showing them what he called his 'little mouse'. This was a steel spring tape-measure which he always carried. He would pull it out a few inches and would tell the child to blow. He then pressed the catch and the mouse tail would disappear. It proved a source of endless delight. He also carried two magnetic bottles in his waistcoat pocket which would not stand up near each other. He was extraordinarily natural and playful with his grandchildren, who adored him. He would take them out all together, pushing the pram with Johanna, taking Charlotte and Alexandra by hand. He contrived regularly to take them to the Zoo.

The Last Years

During the six years which followed his retirement he was, as ever, industrious in pursuit of his research project relating to malignant disease in the South Western Region. He employed all other parts of the week in writing articles, editing books – such as his edition of Müller's diaries – and pursuing his worldwide correspondence. A number of those who had written to him with requests for advice, or questions on intellectual difficulties, were amazed at the full and meticulously written replies. He also continued his full quota of preaching on Sundays and addresses on week-nights (including his Men's Club at the Shaftesbury). One new feature in these years was his introduction of several series of weekly addresses. For example, at Bethesda Chapel, Clifton, during one winter he carried through a successful and well-attended series of addresses on John Bunyan and his writings.

Not many weeks before his death, several friends had commented to each other on an unusual comment made during an address to some young people and, later, reported in a Christian periodical. They hoped that it was not prophetic. He was speaking on the parable of the Talents and clearly had in mind to arouse his youthful audience to a full use of their abilities in Christ's service. He had said 'An absent king does not normally wish to leave his affairs in the hands of rogues or fools' and he had gone on to chide those who are 'too foolish, too lazy, or too timid to use the one talent they have.' He then had continued: 'The Lord can find useful work from youth to old age for servants of Christ. Learn the art of being busy with the Master. The way to be happy when old is to be happy with God ... This lesson must be learnt when young. The Lord Jesus can set you to work and keep you busy until you are buried. And remember that every one of us is immortal until our work is done. Sudden death is better than a lingering illness. Death is the entry into the Father's house "to be in the House of the Lord for ever".'

Rendle Short spent the first week of September 1953 at a conference of the Missionary Study Classes, at Plas Menai, Llanfairfechan. He spoke on several occasions and seemed as active and as alert as ever. He entered into every part of the conference and went for long walks in the region of Snowdon. On 11th September he travelled down with Mrs. Short to Hereford, to stay with some old friends. He had often stayed at the home of Mr. and Mrs. W. Weston before, and was always happy to be there.

His Last Address

On Sunday, as was his custom, A.R.S. attended the worship meeting of the Christian Brethren in Hereford. At the commencement he gave out John Keble's hymn 'New every morning ...'. During the course of the service he gave a short homily from the fiftieth chapter of Isaiah. This was one of the books of the Bible which had been his special study. In closing he emphasized the words of the eleventh verse and spoke of those 'who kindle a fire and walk in the light of it'. He pointed out that the Christian is not left to do that but is able to talk with Christ 'the Light of Life'. His final words were a quotation from 'The Man who stood at the Gate of the Year', with emphasis upon the phrase 'And this will be better to you than light, and safer than a known way'.

In the afternoon he wrote letters as usual, then walked round the garden. He spent a long time, seated in a characteristic attitude in an armchair, with his hands clasped behind his head, giving the son of the house wise counsel about his future academic career and Christian service. During tea he was taken with the first severe stab of pain which betokened a serious heart attack, which proved fatal within twenty-four hours.

He had often spoken publicly of those last hours, which face every one of us, under the title of 'The Last Great Assize'. He remained lucid almost to the end, and characteristically did not complain or grumble. After all, it was his habit not to complain. He had never done so and why should he do so now? *Behind* was a busy life with no moments wasted, a life of useful service and the full utilization of all his talents. Why should he grumble about that? Any failures that lay behind were covered, as he had never tired of saying, by the matchless grace of God. *In front?* Why, in front lay many of his friends, his father, George Müller – and, of course, one Friend Who is greater and closer than any other.

The Farewell

On a bright afternoon the funeral service was held in Bethesda Chapel, Clifton, Bristol, which was filled to overflowing. Representatives were present from many professional organizations and churches from all over the West Country. There were also many citizens of Bristol who had come out of the deep respect and affection which he had evoked by his Christian character, professional integrity and human kindness. The conduct of the service was shared between Dr. Charles Sims (Exeter), Mr. W. M. Capper (Clifton) and Dr. Latimer Short (Weston-super-Mare). For those who knew Rendle Short nothing was more natural than to join heartily in the opening hymn, from Bunyan's well-known lines:

> He who would valiant be
> 'Gainst all disaster,
> Let him in constancy
> Follow the Master.

The last tribute was paid from the text, 'For David, after he had served his own generation by the will of God, fell on sleep, and was laid with his fathers and saw corruption: but he whom God raised again saw no corruption.'* As Mr. Capper reminded the congregation, 'We venture to suggest that no one who really knew Professor Rendle Short could charge him with inconsistency. The more intimately any of us came to know him the more we became convinced of the down-right honesty of his mind and the downright goodness of his life. Throughout his years he was consistently – even passionately – devoted to our Lord Jesus Christ and His holy gospel. His life backed his words by action . . . But I think if Mr. Short were here, he would quietly say to us "It is by the grace of God that I am what I am." "You see", he would add, "it was all due to the Son of God who loved me and gave Himself for me".'

* Acts 13:36, 37.

The remains were committed to the grave at Canford Cemetery in sure and certain hope of the resurrection in our Lord Jesus Christ.

Gloom and sorrow were almost impossible – except that all realized that they were the poorer through the loss of such a truly Christian man. Everyone in the company knew, however, that Rendle Short had simply passed to the full enjoyment of all that he had stood for and taught throughout a spiritually victorious life. It is significant that his good works followed him right up to the end. A citizen, who up to the day of the funeral had been involved in a prolonged quarrel, wrote: 'For the love of Rendle Short I have written a letter of forgiveness.' Another conveyed a message to Mrs. Short that she had taken the first step towards finding peace with God at the graveside.

During the service in Hereford on that last Sunday morning of his life, Rendle Short had quoted from one of his favourite poems, *The Bird on the Bough:*

Like the bird on the bough
That is ready to break,
She feels the branch tremble
But gaily she sings,
What is it to her?
She has wings! She has wings!

This is matched by his thoughts in the final paragraph of *The Bible and Modern Medicine,* the latest edition of which was completed only a few weeks before his death. He wrote:

'When it becomes evident that the earthly pilgrimage is drawing to its close, the Christian soul may permit itself the luxury of dwelling on the visions and unveilings of St. John the Divine, and of seeing with him what lies beyond mortal sight: that blessed country where there is no more pain, and all tears are wiped away; where the New Jerusalem comes down from God out of heaven, where His servants shall serve Him, and they shall see His face. Thoughts like these have drawn the sting of death for a great multitude that no man can number. These passages have inspired the most moving and magnificent prose and poetry in our language, such as the concluding pages of John Bunyan's *Pilgrim's Progress,* both in its first and second parts; and hymns such as "O happy harbour of the Saints" and "Jerusalem the Golden", which, next after the Bible itself, have lightened for millions the sunset, or, shall we say, the dawn of life.'

Appendix I. Main Dates

1880	Born at Bristol (6th January)
1894	To Merchant Venturers' College (Bristol City Scholarship)
1896	To University College, Bristol (Bristol City Scholarship)
1899	To the Bristol General Hospital
1902	At University College Hospital, London
1903–4	Resident Posts at the Bristol General Hospital: House Surgeon, Casualty Officer, House Physician
1905–7	Resident posts at the Bristol Royal Infirmary: House Surgeon and Senior Resident Officer
1907–8	At St. Bartholomew's and Guy's Hospitals (London) and the Tropical School of Medicine
1908–9	Marriage. Unable to go abroad; Locums in General Practice
1909–13	Hon. Surgical Registrar (Non-Resident) at the Bristol Royal Infirmary
1910–14	Demonstrator in Physiology
1913–22	Assistant Hon. Surgeon at the Bristol Royal Infirmary
1914–28	Lecturer in Physiology
1922–33	Honorary Surgeon at the Bristol Royal Infirmary
1933	Professor of Surgery, University of Bristol
1946	Professor Emeritus on retirement
1953	Died at Hereford (14th September)

Academic Qualifications
(London University)

1899	B.Sc. in Geology with first class honours and Gold Medal and Scholarship in Physiology
1900	'Intermediate' (Medicine) with first class honours and Gold Medal and an Exhibition in Physiology; first class honours and Gold Medal in Materia Medica; and first class honours in Anatomy
1903	M.B., B.S., with Gold Medal and Exhibition in Materia Medica, Gold Medal and Scholarship in Medicine, and first class honours in Obstetrics
1904	M.D. with Gold Medal
1908	Diploma of Tropical Diseases, with Distinction
1908	Fellowship of the Royal College of Surgeons

Appendix II: Christian Brethren

The independent churches usually known as 'Christian Brethren' or just 'the Brethren', rose in Ireland during the years 1828–30. This was during a period, following the Napoleonic wars, which was one of great political uncertainty and social distress in Europe.

A remarkable group of men in Dublin, amongst whom were several scholarly graduates of Trinity College, became progressively disillusioned with the formalism, secularism and current lack of vision of the 'established' churches. Eventually they set out hopefully in an endeavour to recapture the simplicity and zeal of the earliest Christians as described in the New Testament. They had no desire, or aim, to start a new sect and for some years confidently expected all enlightened Christians to join with them in their endeavour to ensure a revitalised Christian Church. Taking the Bible alone to be the appointed guide for doctrinal beliefs, ethical conduct and forms of worship, they steadily resisted any modification of its first-hand statements by secondary ecclesiastical traditions or credal formularies.

In common with many other Christians at the time (as for example, the High Church 'Tractarians', or the 'Oxford movement' of Pusey and Keble in the Church of England) they believed that the Second Coming of Christ, and divine judgment on the world, were very imminent. This conviction acted as a strong incentive to energetic action. Hence the movement proved of great evangelistic vitality and it rapidly spread to other parts of the British Isles. Several congregational churches in Plymouth, Bristol and throughout the West Country became attached to the movement, which also attracted a succession of outstanding men, who later pioneered in the spheres of biblical scholarship and exposition, overseas Christian missions and several successful enterprises in other fields.

About the middle of the nineteenth century, however, this promising movement became divided. Its new and hitherto independent churches began to group themselves around two poles of leadership, which represented two different outlooks, and were embodied in two different personalities. One of the ablest of the Dublin leaders, John Nelson Darby, a classical scholar of distinction and of great teaching ability, tended more and more to impose his somewhat imperious and exclusive traits on those parts of the movement which be influenced. He ceased to co-operate either with Christians in the historic denominations or with those within the movement who dissented from his viewpoint and gradually began to require doctrinal conformity to his own particular doctrinal views. His growing exclusivism warped the outlook of his followers, who became increasingly subdivided into mutually exclusive groups. The movement as a whole has tended to be known as 'Plymouth' Brethren because of early association with the town, but the title is not accepted within the movement. The 'open' brethren sometimes choose to be known as 'Christian Brethren' or simply as 'Christians'. The 'exclusive' wing still comprises a wide range of viewpoints, some less extreme than others.

Darby's basic principle and exclusiveness had from the first been opposed by the Bristol assemblies, notably by the philanthropist George Müller and one of their earliest missionaries, Anthony Norris Groves. Müller and Groves ceaselessly advocated that 'all true believers' are members of the Christian Church (as biblically defined) and that the essential bond between them is not the amount of 'light' and Christian doctrinal knowledge which each may possess, but the fact that they have received new 'life' in Christ. In other words, eternal 'life', not 'light', is the essential link between believers. Subsequent history reveals that this more 'open' viewpoint has been the more evangelistically productive and that the policy of the Bristol-type churches has for over a century sent hundreds of missionary-evangelists and gifted Christian teachers into all parts of the world. Their example in these respects has undoubtedly encouraged and inspired other Christians in the various mainline Christian denominations. It was to the latter section of the Christian Brethren that Professor Rendle Short belonged. His own references to the movement will be found on pages 96–98.

Appendix III
Publications by Prof. Arthur Rendle Short
I. Religious Books

The Principles of Christians called 'Open Brethren', 1913 (Pickering & Inglis)

A Modern Experiment in Apostolic Missions, 1919 ('Links of Help' Office, Bolton)

The Historic Faith in the Light of Today, 1922 (Marshall Morgan & Scott) (Jointly with B. Colgrave)

The Bible and Modern Research, 2nd edition, 1933 (Marshall Morgan & Scott)

Modern Discovery and The Bible, 4th edition, 1954 (Inter-Varsity Fellowship)

In the Days of the Prophet Isaiah, 2nd edition, 1948. (Pickering & Inglis)

Why Believe? 5th edition, 1951. (Inter-Varsity Fellowship)

Archaeology gives Evidence, 1st edition, 1951 (Tyndale Press)

Wonderfully Made, 1st edition, 1951 (Paternoster Press)

The Bible and Modern Medicine, 1st edition, 1953 (Paternoster Press)

The Diary of George Müller, 1954 (Pickering & Inglis)

II. Medical Books

The New Physiology in Surgical and General Practice, 1911, 1912, 1914, 1920, 1922

An Index to Prognosis and the End Results of Treatment, 1915, 1918, 1922, 1931. (Editor)

When to advise Operation in General Practice, 1916

The Medical Annual from 1919 to 1953. (Joint Editor)

The Synopsis of Physiology (written with C. I. Ham), 1927, 1936, 1938, 1948

The Causation of Appendicitis, 1946

III. Some Important Articles

Professor Rendle Short contributed some 57 articles to the Medical press, several of them joint-articles. The following are amongst the most important:–

'The After-history of Forty Cases of Epithelioma of the Lip', *Brit. Med. J.* (1910) ii, 426–8.

Hunterian Lecture on 'Changes in the Blood in the Causation of Surgical Shock', *Lancet* (1914) i, 731–7.

'Some Phenomena of Surgical Shock,' *Brit. J. Surg.* (1918–19), 6, 402–8.

'The Causation of Appendicitis,' *Brit. J. Surg.* (1920–21), 8, 171–88.

'Appendicitis: its Causation, Diagnosis and Treatment,' *Lancet* (1925), i, 215–69.

Long Fox Memorial Lecture: 'Ten Years' Progress in Surgical Treatment,' *Bristol Med.-chir. J.* (1929), 46, 243–76.

'Treatment of Gastric and Duodenal Ulcer: Statistical Inquiry,' *Brit. Med. J.* (1931), i, 435–40.

ACKNOWLEDGEMENTS

The authors would like to acknowledge the help and suggestions which they have received from the following in the preparation of the book.

Dr. L. P. Ashton, Mr. E. Bale, Miss P. Z. Bennett, Mrs. F. G. Bergin, Mr. Douglas Brealey, Mr. & Mrs. George Brealey, Prof. F. F. Bruce, Mr. T. J. Butler, Dr. R. J. de Carteret, Mr. Clifford Case, Lt. Col. Winifrede Case, Mr. B. Colgrave, Miss E. Colgrave, Mr. P. Cousins, Miss M. M. B. Denning, Miss E. Ewen, Miss R. Ewen, Dr. H. J. Orr-Ewing, Dr. A. Charles Fisher, Mrs. M. Goodman, Mr. J. Johnson, Mr. Stacey King, Dr. A. W. Langford, Miss Lloyd, Dr. A. E. W. McLachlan, Mr. John McReady, Mrs. W. R. Moore, Mrs. Fletcher Moorshead, Mr. Charles Nightingale, Dr. M. E. J. Packer, Dr. Margaret M. Patterson, Mrs. M. H. Peel, Mrs. A. Pratt, Mr. George E. Price, Mr. A. Pulleng, Mr. J. J. Rose, Mr. P. O. Ruoff, Dr. David S. Short, Dr. Latimer J. Short, Mrs. A. Rendle Short, Prof. C. Rendle-Short, Miss M. Rendle-Short, Dr. T. J. Rendle-Short, Dr. Stephen S. Short, Dr. Charles H. Sims, Mrs. J. Stephen, Mr. W. Stunt, Dr. F. A. Tatford, Mrs. H. Taylor, Lt. Col. R. Y. Taylor, Miss L. S. Toller, Prof. R. Milnes-Walker, Mr. W. Weston, Mrs. G. E. White, and to the following periodicals and their editors: 'Echoes of Service'; 'The Harvester'; 'The Life of Faith'; 'Links of Help'; 'The Witness'.

Special acknowledgements are made to the publishers of books written by Professor Rendle Short for their permission to quote extensively some of the outstanding paragraphs:–

Marshall, Morgan & Scott (London)
Inter-Varsity Press (London)
Pickering & Inglis (Glasgow)
The Paternoster Press (Exeter)
John Wright & Sons (Bristol)

Our thanks are also due to Miss Marjorie Watling for typing the MSS.